HOW THE 'QUY EFFECT' BEGAN . . .

"I had a workbench about ten feet long. On that I had, bolted, a pretty heavy test-bed, a hundredweight or two. In that were two heavy terminals. Between them was clamped my strip of test material. The terminals were connected, via a transformer and a hefty impedance, to a generator. I fed a couple of hundred volts through the strip. It held. It registered zero impedance itself. And then I stepped the voltage up a few more hundred. It still held. Then I really went mad and shoved fifty thousand through it.

"And then there was the explosion . . ."

The Quy Effect

Arthur Sellings

A BERKLEY MEDALLION BOOK
Published by
BERKLEY PUBLISHING CORPORATION

For Chas Kearns

One

The bang that destroyed the silence over Belvedere
Marshes that April evening was the biggest anybody in
the neighborhood had heard for years.

One thing was sure: nobody needed to ring the alarm
in. Sirens and firebells were going like mad. And, though
there was, so far anyway, no fire or other visible aftermath, nobody was in any doubt about where the noise
had come from—Riverside Way.

For all its grandiloquent name, Riverside Way was a
poorly maintained road which had been built only to
serve a cluster of small to medium-size factories and
which petered out into the marshes a few yards beyond
them. It was in that direction that the crowds set off,
on foot, on bicycles and in cars, impeding—to the curses
of ambulance men, firemen and civil defense workers—
the rescue vehicles that were also converging on the incident.

Thrillseekers and rescue workers alike found it without difficulty. Under a fitfully moonlit sky, half the
Hypertronics factory lay in ruins. It was the last factory
in the road, a relative newcomer of a few years before.
Now the wincingly-green glass front of the office block,
stark in the light of clustering headlamps, was cracked
across in several places. One of the squat white towers
that had surmounted it was lying in the road. The other
was leaning tipsily, the flag of Hypertronics flapping like

5

a battle-torn banner from a flagpole that had cracked in half without utterly parting.

One end of the factory itself was roofless; the rest still had cover, but the explosion had ripped out one wall and the base of the cantilever with it, collapsing the roof. At two points, taller machines poked up through it.

Mercifully, it being a Saturday night, no night shifts were being worked in this or any of the neighboring factories. The latter—notably King-Size Popcorn, Eyebright Optical Lenses and Hilo Pocketbooks Ltd.—seemed to have escaped serious damage; though gaping windows and, here and there, gashed concrete bore witness to the explosion that had wrecked Hypertronics.

The night watchman had escaped unhurt; he had been sharing a pot of tea with the watchman of King-Size when the big bang had happened—a chance that had almost certainly saved his life. But he was careful not to mention that fact to the rescuers as he led the way past the office block and the factory to the center of the explosion, the remotest of the scattered buildings of Hypertronics.

Only the concrete floor and stumps of walls, like the excavated ruins of some ancient city, gave any indication that there had been a building here at all.

"What was in here?" the control officer of the fire service asked the watchman. "Any explosives or dangerous work going on?"

"Only what I've been trying to tell you," said the watchman, whose babbled words had been silenced so far by the control officer. "There wasn't nothing explosive, not that I know of. And if there had've been I'd have been told. I know there was some kind of hush-hush work going on in here, but—"

"Hush-hush? You do mean dangerous, then? Was there any equipment left on over the weekend?"

"I was just going to tell you," the watchman said testily. "Somebody was working in here."

"This evening, you mean?"

6

"Course I mean this evening."

"Who?"

"Mr. Quy."

"Quy?" The fire officer had shown no emotion at the news that somebody had been on the spot, but his eyebrows lifted slightly now at the unusual name. His pen hovered over a clipboard. "How do you spell that?"

"Q-U-Y."

"And you pronounce it like that—Kwye?"

"That's the way *he* always did."

"First names?"

"I don't remember right now. But what the hell are you bothering with details like that for now? Why don't you try and—"

He stopped, interrupted not by words but by the cold, unemotional gaze of the fire officer as it traversed the space where once there had been a building. And the watchman realized that he had protested only out of loyalty. He had liked old Quy. He was like one of the men, with none of the snootiness of the rest of the high-ups. He used to eat in the workers' canteen, on the few occasions when he seemed to remember meals, as if he despised the tablecloths and napkins of the staff room—or the other members of the staff.

But he wouldn't be seen in the canteen again—or anywhere else—the watchman thought, as he followed the gaze of the fire officer. Bricks and concrete and steel girders had vanished utterly. What chance could flesh and blood have had? The watchman shivered at the thought; there wasn't a trace of either left. No gruesome smear of blood or tatter of overall coat even to show that old Quy had been in here when it had happened. But he must have been. When old Quy stayed on to work, he *worked*. *He* didn't go off for cups of tea.

Across the shattered landscape came a fireman with a walkie-talkie.

"A casualty just been found, sir."

The fire officer followed him. The watchman hurried after them.

7

A hundred yards or more they squelched across the marsh, pushing a way through the crowds, till they reached the ambulance men. A white-coated doctor was kneeling over a figure sprawled in the grass. The light was dim here at the limit of the headlamps and the floodlights that the rescue men had rigged up.

"My gawd!" the watchman said. "All in one piece!"

"He's all right," the doctor said. "Fractured scapula and multiple bruising. But nothing serious, no damage to organs that I can make out, and no hemorrhaging. Don't suppose anybody knows who he is? Looks like a tramp to me."

The man looked like one. The rescue workers had swathed him in blankets against loss of body heat in shock. The doctor had pulled it aside for his examination, revealing a gaunt figure clad in a tattered, checked shirt and a pair of baggy rat-colored corduroy trousers held up by a large safety pin. The face above the clothes was old and lined, prickled with white stubble and surmounted by a shock of yellow-white hair. Lying there, his eyes shut, he could easily have been taken for a down-and-out sleeping off a bout with the meth bottle.

But the watchman leaped indignantly to his defense.

"Tramp!" he echoed. "That's Mr. Quy." He turned to the fire officer. "The one I was telling you about."

"You *do* know him, then?" said the doctor.

"He's some kind of research worker at the factory," said the fire officer.

"You mean—?" The doctor was young; he looked even younger in his surprise. His head jerked in the direction of the wrecked buildings. "You mean—he was *in there*?"

"So was I," the watchman lied, thinking it time he got his own story in order. "I must have been protected by a wall." He'd check and find a likely one before old Maddox and the rest of the bosses turned up, as they were bound to do before long.

"But *you* weren't blown three hundred feet," the doc-

8

tor said. "This man must have been on the site of the explosion to have been thrown this far."

"Course he was," said the watchman. "He was the one who caused it."

"Careful," the fire officer said, turning on him sharply. "That hasn't been established yet. My report on an incident is confidential, but just you mind what you say to other people."

"But it must have been him. I know it wasn't me, and we were the only two here tonight."

"Well, it's a miracle," the doctor said. "This soft ground must have cushioned his fall. Even so—"

He shook his head wonderingly, then nodded to the ambulance men. They had strapped up the casualty's shoulder; now they wrapped the gaunt form back in the blankets, laid it on a stretcher and were about to hoist it when the eyes flickered open. They were bloodshot and red-rimmed. The old man's lips moved.

The doctor bent over him, listening for a moment. Then he straightened and gestured to the stretcher-bearers to take the casualty away to the ambulance that waited, its blue lamp flashing, at the end of the road.

"What did he say?" the fire officer asked.

The young doctor looked at him and grinned. "It sounded suspiciously like 'Whisky' to me."

Two

"The phone's ringing, dear."

"Eh? Lord, no! Not on a Sunday morning!" He turned away from the early morning light that squinted through the curtains.

9

"It *could* be the Ministry."

The word jerked his eyes open. "It had better not be anyone else," he grumbled as he got stiffly out of bed. He flung on a dressing gown, groped into slippers and shuffled downstairs.

"Fortis three nine double-o."

"Who is that, please?"

It was a woman's voice. Even in his only barely awake state, he was sure he didn't recognize it. It wasn't anybody from the Ministry, he was sure of that.

He told her—curtly.

"I'm sorry, Mr Key," said the voice. "I must have been given a wrong number. I'm trying to locate a Mr. Preston Quy."

He sighed heavily. "That's me."

"Oh? Oh yes, I see. You pronounce it Key."

"It's an old French name," he told her testily. "Who are you, and what do you want at this unearthly hour of the morning?"

A half-minute later he put the receiver down.

"Who was it, dear?" came his wife's voice from upstairs, a second after the terminal *ting*.

"It's father." His voice was annoyed. "He's in the hospital."

"Father's what? All right. I'm coming down."

In a few moments she did so, a frilly yellow negligée only exaggerating her square dumpy figure.

"Whose?"

"Mine. He's in the hospital. Do they think *everybody* keeps hospital hours?"

"Oh, the poor dear. It must be serious for them to ring you up this early. What is it—his heart at last? Only the other day I was thinking—"

"Heart? That's a good one! He's got a heart made of chrome steel and vulcanized rubber. No, the crazy old coot's gone and blown himself up."

"Oh *no*! We must go and see him. Which hospital is he at?"

"The Erith General."

"Erith? Where's that?"

"A dreary place the other side of creation. The other side of London, anyway. Trust *him*. And there's no need for us to go haring out there. He's all right—just a cracked collarbone and bruises."

She gave him a sharp glance. "All *right*? Fractures can be serious at his age. Complications can set in. Just how old *is* he?"

"Oh, I don't know. Seventy-odd. Seventy-two, I think."

"Well, we must certainly go and see him as soon as we can today. I'll get the coffee on."

She retreated to the kitchen. Preston sighed, shook his head, then followed her.

He sat down at the breakfast table morosely, looking out over the garden. It was large, like the house. The trees were budding and birds were flittering between their branches in the level rays of the early morning sun. He lit a cigarette, conscious of his wife's disapproving glance. Another morning she would have protested at his lighting one before breakfast, but today the glance melted into a permissive half-smile.

He was stubbing it out when coffee was set in front of him. His wife sat down with him.

"I'd like a cigarette too," she said.

He gave her one and lit it, with another for himself, making a mental resolve to cut out his usual mid-morning cigarette to compensate. One couldn't be blamed for smoking if one had a responsible job like his, but ten a day was what he kept it down to, even on the hardest days. He didn't even let a fussing Minister push up his quota. That would have been a moral defeat.

"Why do you hate your father?" his wife said suddenly.

He blinked at her, surprised and indignant. "*Hate* him? I don't hate him." He took a deep drag at his cigarette, feeling less annoyed with his wife than with the fact that his hand was trembling slightly. Then he shrugged. "Perhaps I do. And perhaps not. I've tried often enough. And with enough reason to. But it's the other way round. *He* hates *me*—he always has."

"Oh no—you *can't* say that. I know there's not much love lost between you, but he gave you your education, at least. You wouldn't have got where you are today without that."

He laughed hollowly. "Education! Fat lot of education he ever gave me."

"Oh, I know you won scholarships and things, dear. All the same—"

"All the same nothing. It was my mother who scrimped and saved to see that I got proper tuition, saw me through University. It wasn't like today then—the grants were pretty meager."

She looked at him pensively. "You have told me before. About your mother. But you've never talked much about your father. Only when he's got into some kind of a scrape. And then you only get angry—"

"Who's being angry?"

"Short, anyway. And *hurt*. I know you went through some tough times, but—"

"Tough? No, they weren't all that tough. No tougher in the thirties than they were for a lot of other people. And I was still only a kid when the war broke out. During the depression years we had it better than a lot—and we could have had it better still. If the old man hadn't been such an old bas—"

"*Preston!*"

"I didn't say it, did I?" In fact, he was going to say *basket*, one of the euphemisms with which he hedged himself round. He grimaced. "All right, pull up the black leather couch, if that's what you want."

She flinched from the imputation of feminine inquisitiveness. "I just don't want to see you getting yourself all upset. Any time your father's name comes up you really do get terribly agitated."

"Perhaps I'm just mad at myself for not being able to forget the past. Perhaps my control isn't good enough.

12

If I tell you, perhaps you'll realize then why I never talk about it much.

"My father . . . I don't know where to begin. Perhaps it's really a kind of philosophical thing, outraged beliefs and all that. I'm not a religious man, you know that, Doris, but I do believe that if a man's on this earth he should do his utmost to strive to—well, fulfill himself."

"It's strange that you should make that judgment on your father—of all people. I think he's the most dedicated man I've ever met. He hasn't wasted his talents, surely?"

"Name one thing that he ever followed through."

"Well—there was his water softener. Ours is still as good as new. And his kitchen slicing machine. There's nothing quite as good on the market, even now."

"Oh—the great Universal Housewife's Friend! I remember printing the cards for them on a ramshackle printing machine he rigged up. I was about eight at the time. He hawked them round the shops. But they're only gadgets."

"*Good* gadgets."

"All right, but gadgets. They were just things he threw off to make money when he needed it. If he'd protected them well enough, either one of them would probably still be paying royalties now and my mother would be living in some kind of comfort in a little cottage in Sussex, or somewhere, instead of—"

His voice broke off.

"You can't blame your mother's death on him!"

"Can't I? Sometimes the spirit gives up the struggle, just like the body."

His wife changed tack quickly. "Anyway, you can't measure a man's dedication by his worldly success. Your father's a *scientist*."

"My father's a *tinkerer*. Always has been and always will be. The original Man With the Grasshopper Mind. Do you remember those ads?"

"*Why* are you so bitter? You've told me yourself that he pioneered a lot of things."

"That's just what I mean. Somewhere in him there

13

was once a tremendous mind. I always used to think so, anyway. I worshipped that man—that mind. Oh yes, he pioneered a lot of things, but you won't find one mention of him in the histories of any of them. Look up the history of television, you'll find the names of Baird and Zworykin. You'll even find an honored place for Nipkow back in the eighteen-eighties. But Quy? Not a word. Rocketry? Goddard, Ley, von Oberth, Tsiolkowski, Esnault-Pelterie." He smiled bitterly. "I think the *Mid-Sussex Express* mentioned the name of Quy when he burned down a sizable piece of Ashdown Forest back in the twenties."

"Science isn't all honors."

"Don't you think I know that? You won't find *my* name mentioned anywhere either—except in inter-departmental memos."

"You're young yet."

"I'm forty-three. I chose my career with my eyes open. I don't fancy I shall take up original research again after all these years. I'm not complaining. Science is teamwork these days. The administrator, the organizer, is just as important as the man at the bench, probably more so. Research is too complicated now. The day of the lone inventor is over. You need too much money, too many minds working with you, too many technicians working *for* you.

"But the old man could never work as a member of a team. He was always the lone pioneer. I grew up in a world where there was still room for the breed. Baird, Fleming—the radio valve Fleming, not the penicillin one —Rutherford. Even Rutherford was one of a team—the kingpin of it, but a team man all the same. He couldn't have achieved what he did without the backing of a university. It was already a dying race. Fleming was a part of history then."

"But the other Fleming—the penicillin one. Wasn't he postwar?"

"Wartime. Another team man. A hospital laboratory, not a shed in the garden. The shed in the garden has had

14

it. So has the cellar with apparatus draped round the walls. When I was a kid that was the kind of place my father spent all his time in. When he wasn't going the rounds trying to sweet-talk somebody into investing a packet in the latest wild scheme he'd cooked up. Oh, my father wasn't a man of single talents. He had a smooth tongue—and quite a way with women. Or he thought he had."

His wife laughed incredulously. "Oh no, Press, you can't make him out such an old devil as that! I've only met him two or three times, but he always seemed quite a benign old soul to me."

"Didn't I just say he had a way with women? You remember when he had pneumonia that time, and you thought I was heartless not to have him here to convalesce?"

"You mean—you surely don't seriously mean—?"

"Don't be ridiculous. Not that I'd put that past him. If he needed money he would have been after your private account like a shot, and no holds barred. I'm not joking. But he wouldn't have wasted any time getting round the neighbors. That was the main reason I wouldn't let him set foot in this place. That and a peculiar aversion to having the house blown up around my ears."

"*Thank* you. So you were more worried about the house and the neighbors."

He lifted his eyes to heaven. "I mean *you*. And Alan. And, all right, the house too. I've made too many sacrifices to get a house in this kind of neighborhood to want to go through it again in a hurry."

"Alan still sees him, you know."

"Yes, I do know. You can't very well stop a kid seeing his own grandfather. But that's another reason I wouldn't have him here to live. Being in contact with a corrupting influence like that two or three times a year is one thing, having said corrupting influence in residence is quite another. But the main reason I've never asked him is that he would have laughed in my face. I've been humiliated by him too many times. If I'd pleaded with

15

him he might have given in, but his unbearability, his dangerousness, his power of scandalizing the neighborhood would have been in direct ratio to my pleading. I *know*."

"But he's old now. You're letting memories of the past obscure the present—and your judgment."

"Am I? I can remember the happy times too. You're quite right; he wasn't quite such an old devil. Not all the time, anyway. He knew all right what a time he gave my mother, and he would try to redeem himself. When he made a killing he'd come home with all kinds of gifts for mother and me. He wasn't mean with money. He just didn't care about it, except what he needed to finance his experiments.

"Some of the things he brought home were ridiculous. He arrived once in a pantechnicon with a grand piano. And once he brought me a boa constrictor—a live one. Another time he came home and showered my mother with gold sovereigns. She was sitting at the table—I shall never forget *that* night—it was covered with a green baize cloth. And we only had candlelight because the electricity had been turned off for nonpayment. We hadn't seen father for weeks, and my mother looked up at him, trying to look stern and accusing. Heaven knows she had cause enough to be stern with him. And then he just lifted up this leather bag and showered her with sovereigns.

"At times like that we thought that everything was going to be happy ever after, that he had come to his senses. But he went off again the next day, and we didn't see him for nearly a year. And the sovereigns didn't last for ever, even if they were worth about thirty shillings each at that time. There came a time when we had to make a moonlight flit.

"How old was I?—about eight, I think—and I didn't know what a moonlight flit was. I didn't know the name for it, I mean. But I always thought it was funny that we used to move more often by night than by day. And *move*! We never stayed in one place for long. So much for my education! I had almost as many schools as hot dinners. And hot dinners were a luxury. One week we'd live on pheasant or Scotch salmon—'We've got to live in a manner befitting the Great Scientist,' he'd say—the next week it would be bread and margarine."

"At least you got the Scotch salmon and the pheasant."

"Oh yes, it was the great romantic life, you mean? It wasn't. There was too much heartbreak and loneliness for my mother. When we had to move, after the sovereigns episode, you know my mother actually lost all trace of my father. In the circumstances she could hardly leave a forwarding address. We might never have seen him again if he hadn't sought *us* out. He was flat broke, of course, otherwise I'm pretty sure he wouldn't have bothered. There was a terrible row. He wanted to know where all the money had gone that he had given my mother.

"The only quiet time we had was during the war. We were down in the country—Somerset. My father was working at a secret factory down there. Ironical, isn't it? I mean, taking a war to give us a bit of peace and security. I think the old man found peace of mind too. It was the only time, anyway, he seemed to be able to work as one of a team."

"Was that when he was awarded the M.B.E.?"

"Don't remind me of it. When the war finished, that was just one more weapon in his armory. That M.B.E. must have been flashed around half the board rooms in England by now—and half the saloon bars. I don't mention these things to you, but more than once my father's been a heck of a nuisance to me and my career. He tried to get me to use my influence to get him into a branch of my own Ministry, to carry out research vital to the country—he claimed. I refused point-blank. Afterwards I found him working there under an assumed name. You know what security's like in *our* outfit. There he was, as bold as brass, a whole faked history in the dossier, using the Ministry time and resources to work on some harebrained scheme of his own. I nearly had a heart attack. If I showed him up, he'd have landed in prison—

17

M.B.E. or no M.B.E.—and I'd have been out on my ear."

"How long ago was this?"

"About seven years ago. You remember, when you wanted Alan to go to that expensive prep school in Hampstead and you thought I was being mean about the money?"

"Oh, *then*." Her eyes widened. "You don't mean—"

"Of course." Self-justification and bitterness were mixed in his voice. "I had to *buy* him out. It cost me five hundred pounds."

"Oh, Press, I had no idea."

"I didn't worry you with it. He's my father. Perhaps you realize now just what kind of a father he's been. And that if I did hate him I'd have every excuse. But I tell you, it's the other way around. He hasn't so much hated me as *despised* me. He always has, even when I was a wide-eyed kid, worshipping him despite all he put my mother through. To me he was the Great Scientist. I dreamed of following in his footsteps."

"But I think I sensed even then that there was something lacking in my father's abilities—not that I would ever have dreamed of admitting it. I knew he was weak on theory. He never had any formal education. He hasn't got a single letter after his name, except that M.B.E. By the time he got that, my eyes were a bit more open. By then it was too late. I was about the same age as Alan is now and I had committed myself. I've no regrets on that score. I might have been a lousy lawyer."

"I'm sure you would have been a very good lawyer."

He shrugged away the stereotyped loyalty. "I thought it was just his way of bringing me up—you know, treat 'em mean and keep 'em keen. An act—until I took my place by his shoulder. Forgive the shining image; I was only a kid. But it wasn't an act. He just didn't need me. Yet he never followed through on a single thing. He dropped working on rockets before the war, when it was obvious that the Germans were getting government support and romping ahead. He gave up after a couple of attempts to get our government interested.

"Before then he pioneered television. I found some papers of his once—tucked behind a pipe in the toilet—and they were notes dating from the early twenties—outlining a kind of cathode-ray tube. That was when Baird was working on a cardboard disc with holes in. I never knew why he dropped TV. Perhaps that was when he dreamed up a basic jet engine. Or a patent tie clip. It might just as easily have been one as the other.

"You see, no perspective. Because he never had the education to give him a perspective. And it just didn't register on him when I got scholarships. On one of the few occasions when he opened up with me—it must have been after he'd had a few drinks—he told me a story about Henry Ford. About how Ford wanted to produce glass for his cars in a continuous strip process. His experts said it couldn't be done. So he called a clerk out of the sales office, somebody out of accounts, and a hand off the shop floor and told them to find a way. And they found it because they had never learned enough to know that it couldn't be done. That was one of my father's favorites. I heard him tell it to several people. Once to a headmaster of mine, to put him in his place."

He sighed. "No, my father had talent all right. But he never learned how to use it."

"You keep talking in the past tense."

"I'm talking about the past. All right, I know what you mean. But he'll never make anything of his life now. There isn't one of the fields that he pioneered in that hasn't gone way past any theory he may have had. Anyway, that's the story of my Life With Father. And once is enough."

He turned to look out of the window. The early morning sun had given way to rain. He turned back with sudden ferocity. "Except that one day I'll tell you why I could *really* hate my father."

"But—" his wife began, when a third voice interrupted them.

19

"Why *hul*-lo."

It was Alan. His father recognized the pronunciation as a brand mark of a current TV comic, uttered with all the unctuous emphasis of the prototype plus the energy of a sixteen-year-old. Preston was approaching the age when the energy of the young hurt physically. He winced.

"What are we all doing up so bright and early?" Alan inquired. "I heard voices raised in unseemly discourse." He caught a quick glance between his father and mother. "It's all right, I couldn't make out a single word, if you were talking about sex or something."

"*Alan*," said his mother.

His father told him, "We were talking about your grandfather Adolphe. He's in hospital."

"Oh *no*. What's wrong with him?"

"It's all right, he'll survive. He just broke a bone or two. He blew himself up."

"I bet he was trying out something fantastic."

"Knowing your grandfather, he probably forgot to read the diagram."

"Grandfather doesn't read diagrams—"

"Exactly."

"He *makes* them. *Ee*! When are we going to see him?"

"*We* are not going to see him at all."

His wife interposed. "Aren't you going today?"

"*I* am, yes. But there's no need for you to come too, Doris."

"But—"

"I'd prefer to see him on my own," he said meaningly. "As for you, Alan, you can go and see him if you want to. But not with me today. And I'd better warn you that it's the other side of London—Erith."

"So what? I can go down on the hovercraft service. It stops at Erith."

"You may go down by any route you wish. But kindly desist from saying *So what*? It's neither polite nor grammatical."

Three

By the time Preston Quy had shaved and dressed, had breakfast and got the '69 Humber out, it had stopped raining and the roads were already dry under an unusually warm sun for April. He had intended to go through the Dartford Tunnel and double back to Erith, out it seemed that half of North London was heading for the Essex coast. Half-an-hour's holdup made him change his mind and turn southward for Blackfriars.

The roads were emptier here, but as soon as he was over the bridge he got caught up in another sluggish stream. Half of South London seemed to be on *its* way to the Kent and Sussex coasts.

He swore and tried to take evasive action through backstreets. Three cul-de-sacs and a Sunday street market convinced him that patience among the herd was the only course. He reached the hospital at half-past twelve in a foul temper and had to kick his heels until lunch time was over. He bought a large bunch of daffodils from a barrow at the gate and went in.

He asked for his father at the office, feeling the usual small sense of defeat at pronouncing Quy in his father's English way.

"Oh yes, the old gentleman who was admitted last night. He's in Ward Seventeen. Take the lift to the third floor. Turn left. It's at the end of the corridor."

Preston followed the directions and found a door marked 17, smaller than the usual ward swing-door. But that was his father all right, propped up in bed and

21

visible through the glass panel. *Trust him,* Preston thought as he went in. This was a private ward.

His father, in striped hospital pajamas, his left arm strapped across them, looked up from a copy of the *News of the World.*

"Well, if it isn't my flesh and blood. I expected the chef. I complained about the standard of the food. One doesn't pay for a private ward and expect to get National Health cod and parsley sauce."

"*One*?" Preston became uneasily aware of the careful neutrality of the word. "Look here—you're not expecting me to—"

"I'm not expecting you to do anything. That's all taken care of."

"Don't think," Preston muttered hurriedly, "that I don't want you to have every comfort, but we pay enough taxes for hospitals, so I firmly believe in—"

"I told you it's taken care of. Or will be." His father seemed to have just noticed the flowers. "Wait a minute, are you sure you got the right message?" He cackled derisively.

A nurse came in just then. Old Quy grabbed the flowers and presented them to her, bowing slightly from his sitting-up position. "Here we are, my dear, a tribute from an admirer."

The nurse, a halfway pretty redhead, smiled. "I'm sure they were brought for you, Mr. Quy. Let me put them in a vase."

Old Quy's bright eyes followed her as she arranged them in a vase, which she set by the window sill.

"While you're here," he called, "have a look at the radiator tap, will you? It seems chilly in here." He licked his lips as she bent down, her stiff uniform swaying out to reveal an ample stretch of thigh.

"There's nothing wrong with the radiator, Mr. Quy," she said. "It's full on." She took his temperature and went out.

"*Ooh,* did you see that leg?" old Quy enthused. "Black stockings do a hell of a lot for a girl. Weird, isn't it—

22

they're the uniform of sisters of mercy and can-can dancers, Salvation Army girls and the other sisters of mercy. A small demonstration of the dialectical nature of the universe, eh?"

"You don't get any better," his son told him.

"A man's got to have a bit of recreation, cooped up in a place like this, hasn't he? Still, I shan't be here long. Where's Alan? Haven't seen him for months."

"He's studying hard. He takes his O-Levels this year. But no doubt he'll be coming down to see you. I thought it best to come on my own today."

The old man cocked his head. "Why?"

"Well—in case you were in any kind of a jam or—"

"Jam?" He said it as if he had never heard of the word. "Far from that being the case, let me tell you, son, that I've just discovered the greatest thing since the steam engine."

Preston suppressed a sigh. "How do you discover anything blowing yourself up?"

"You can't make an omelette without breaking eggs. Getting yourself blown up is as good a way as any of getting your eyes opened for you. I was testing the latest sample of a complex molecule with about a hundred times the current it would have to take in normal operation. It held up to that point. Though I must confess that I didn't expect quite so violent a reaction. You wait till Maddox comes to see me. His eyes will pop out. I'll make his fortune—and mine."

Like any other hospital visitor, Preston felt he ought to make conversation, but he hated himself for saying, "Who's Maddox? And what have you been experimenting with this time?"

He hated himself even more when his father said, "It's all very hush-hush yet, my boy. D'you think I'd let drop a hint to any of your mob? I'm going to get this tied up so tight that the government will have to pay a fortune for the use of it. I had enough belting my brains out for the government during the war. By rights I should have got fifty thousand, tax-free, out of them for the work I

23

did then. And all I got was a bloody medal. I'm going to get my own back this time. I'll squeeze 'em till the pips squeak."

Preston could not surpress a heavy sigh now. He had heard it all before. "Okay, father. If you can win out against the Treasury, good luck to you. But is there anything I can do for you now?"

"No, nothing at all," the old man said airily.

"Sure? Books, papers, anything?"

"Nope."

There was a long and awkward silence.

"Well, I'll be off, then. Oh, Doris sends her love, of course."

As he reached the door, his father called out, "Oh, there is just one small thing you can do."

Preston turned. "Yes?"

The old man grinned. "Close that radiator down a bit. It's got very stuffy in here."

Preston grimaced but did as he was asked, then left, shaking his head sadly.

A few minutes later old Quy rang the bell. But it was a cold-eyed sister who came.

"No, Mr. Quy, what is it this time? Don't imagine that having a private ward entitles you to jab that button every five minutes. We have our own remedies for awkward patients, let me warn you."

"The radiator's gone cold."

The sister sniffed suspiciously and knelt down primly to investigate, showing nothing. It wouldn't have been much of a treat anyway, Quy thought.

"The valve was half shut," the sister told him curtly. "It's fully open now." She halted by the door. "And if I catch you out of bed closing it again I'll put Plan A into immediate operation. That's cascara every three hours and a cold blanket bath twice a day. Really, Mr. Quy, I'm surprised at you."

"What, at my age, you mean? I'm a late developer, sister."

24

"No, at the age of that gag," she told him acidly. She stepped aside as the door opened.

"Ah, Maddox!" said Quy enthusiastically. "You've got the news then. I got somebody to phone the works as soon as I realized. Great, isn't it?"

"Great? *Great*? Let me tell you"—Maddox broke off at a glare from the sister.

"You mustn't excite the patient," she told him. "Are you a relative?"

"If I ever thought that I could be related to that son of a—" Maddox stopped and coughed. "Don't worry about your patient, sister. I'm the only one who'll need treatment—for blood pressure."

"If he gets too excited," Quy said, "I'll just push the button."

The sister sniffed, glared again and departed.

"Come and sit down, my dear chap," said Quy. "They put armchairs in the private rooms, I'll say that for them, not those horrible hard old things in the general ward. You might as well get value for your money, eh?"

"*My* money?"

"Well, the company's."

"If you think the company's going to pay a penny for your comfort, you must be raving mad. Have you seen the factory?"

"Not since last night. It was all right, the last I remember of it. But I gather there was an explosion. I see there's a bit about it in the papers. Well, I'm sorry if my little research hut got damaged, but the insurance will take care of that. You *are* insured, of course?"

"Yes, we're insured, Quy. But it wasn't just a matter of your research building. Half the factory is demolished, and the other half won't be fit to work in for weeks. Our stockroom doesn't exist any more and its contents are a hundred percent write-off. We may be insured, but our customers can't fill in the circuits of their computers and radios with insurance money. They need components, and they'll get them elsewhere."

"Well, I can't hold myself responsible for your company's insurance cover or the efficiency of its service department. I wasn't hired for that."

"I've been busy searching my brains, since I was hauled away from a cosy fireside late last night, for the reason you *were* hired."

"Always a joker, eh, Maddox? Well, you haven't got a thing to worry about. That last sample did the trick."

"It certainly did," Maddox said grimly.

"*Pah*! That was only a regrettable side effect. I just overloaded it, that's all. Maybe I did get a bit carried away—in more ways than on, eh?—but I'd been working solidly for forty-eight hours. Don't you see the mere fact of the blowout shows that it was a success? If it hadn't been, the thing would simply have given up at the first few watts through it—the same as the others."

"With successes like yours, who wants failures?" Maddox waved a weary hand. "All right, I get the point. That particular sample must have been taking a lot of power before it blew out. But it didn't just blow out—it blew *up*. Maybe you were using too small a section for the load you put on it, but the whole idea behind this misbegotten venture was to find a superconductor that would work—and be safe. That means it would have to have a capacity way above normal working."

"I was using a strip twenty centimeters by five by one. I put fifty thousand volts through it."

"You *what*! At what amperage? No, don't tell me, otherwise I'll be pushing that button right now."

"That's the point. I was working it far beyond any required tolerance."

"But it *exploded*."

"So does a boiler when it's overheated. Does that mean we have to scrap boilers?"

"You can fit a safety valve to a boiler."

"And you can fit a cutout to this."

"Cutout!" Maddox snorted. "And how do you measure when you're approaching the danger point? *What* do you measure it in?"

26

"Details," Quy said contemptously. "I can easily iron out the bugs in it."

"You'll do no such thing," Maddox told him flatly. "As from this moment any connection between you and Hypertronics is severed."

"I'm not sure that a contract can legally be either made or terminated on the Lord's day," Quy said calmly. "I'll have to get advice."

"You'll have to get advice, all right. We had an extraordinary meeting of the board this morning. We agreed that the only satisfaction we could salvage from the wreckage was to sue you for willful damage to the tune of around a million pounds. The writ will state the exact amount."

"*A million*! That's a good one. I haven't got a million farthings."

"Then we'll bankrupt you. And let me say that nothing could give me greater pleasure."

"What a nice loathsome commercial mind you have, Maddox. You're forgetting one small detail."

"I am, am I?"

"Yes," said Quy cheerfully. "I've been bankrupt for years. In fact, I've been bankrupt more times in my life than you've chased a secretary round a filing cabinet."

"You're not going to rile me, Quy. And you're not going to mitigate the pleasure of Hypertronics in general, and me in particular. We're going to sue you. We're going to show you up for the maniac you are. We'll hire a team of investigators to check on those credentials you gave us, for a start. Don't think we can't get back at you somewhere. *You're* forgetting one small detail, too. Maybe you are a man of straw—"

"Ooh, we're full of lovely commercial phrases."

"This isn't just a matter of pounds, shillings, and pence. If we can prove false pretenses—and I'm pretty sure we'll be able to—it won't be just a case for the civil courts, but for the criminal ones. And you won't be able to wriggle out of that—you'll go behind bars."

27

"Now, wait, Maddox. You're being a bit too hasty now."

"I thought that would make you change your tune."

"Not at all. It's about time you changed yours. Can't you see the possibilities in this? Whatever false pretenses you think you can prove around the edges—and you'll have a hard job proving to any court that a man's selling himself is a crime—the central proposition I came to you with was a perfectly valid one. It was that you would finance me in research into superconductors at ordinary temperatures. My starting point was the BCS theory, backed up by Fritz London's speculations and the further theories of Little of Stanford. The program was impeccably based."

"I've heard it all before, Quy. I might as well tell you that the board were getting mighty suspicious of you weeks before all this—when you put in those inflated figures for outside computer work."

"Inflated? You'd better be careful how you choose your words. Those computer programs were completely necessary and the figures were true ones."

"They were also well above your authorized budget for the project. So we had Curtis check all research details available, past and present, in the field. And he couldn't find that you were doing anything that hasn't been duplicated elsewhere, in some form or another."

"*Duplication*! My god, Maddox, duplication has been the keynote in science ever since Leibnitz and Newton discovered calculus simultaneously. And for all the ages before, probably. Probably a dozen people scattered through the world invented the wheel at the same time. Don't talk to me about duplication. I've had enough credit snatched from me before by duplication."

He laughed hollowly.

"And now, I turn up with the answer first, and all you can do is threaten lawsuits! It *worked,* Maddox, can't you get that into your head? I *was* breaking new ground. I knew I was getting close to it. Perhaps I was too busy to keep your office properly informed, but I didn't want any holdups. How else do you think an explosion that size could have happened unless that little bit of material of mine *had* absorbed everything I'd fed it up to that point? And then broken down and released it all in one go? Come on, you tell me. You're a scientist—or you were one before you got bogged down in the commercial details. You tell me."

"That's beside the point."

"Oh no, it isn't. You'll have to prove just what form my alleged willful destruction took. And in so doing I fancy that you'd only prove my case for me. And, if it comes to lawsuits, let me remind you that I have a contract with Hypertronics, and I haven't given you the slightest grounds for tearing it up. Furthermore, on a level to which I must confess I would hesitate to stoop, unless—" he fixed the other with a beady eye—"I was forced to, let me point out that I was a workman for the company and, as such, entitled to the protection of the various Workmens' Compensation Acts."

"You're stark, staring mad!"

"Am I? I think I'm a reasonable man, if you handle me properly. *I* don't want to force the issue. All I want is my job and my laboratory back. So you'd better get the salvage squads onto that little job as top priority. *And* the necessary allocations out of the insurance money. Because as soon as I can escape from this boneyard I'll be presenting myself at the Hypertronics gates."

Maddox got to his feet, his face twitching. By the time he reached the door, he seemed to have regained control, if barely.

"You'll be wasting your time. They'll be barricaded."

"In that case," said Quy sweetly, "I'll bring a battering ram. Or a ballista."

Four

The sister came in at nine o'clock that evening. Quy was hunched up in bed, his left arm stiff in its sling, the other clutching his skinny knees. His face drawn in the small circle of light from his bed lamp, he stared gloomily out of the window into the darkness beyond.

"Mr. *Quy*. Now come along. I told you half an hour ago it was lights out. You must get some rest."

"I don't want rest. Leave me alone, woman, I'm thinking."

The sister sniffed. "Some pretty unpleasant thoughts, too, by the look on your face."

He turned his head, leering. "I think I'm pregnant, sister."

"I think you're crazy."

"A seventy-year gestation with a monster inside me. And it's stuck. You'd look pretty pained, too. What do you recommend, sister—a cesarean?"

The sister made a grab for his pillow and jerked it back. She held up the pill triumphantly. "I thought so! I'll settle you, my lad."

She came back with a pill as big as his eyeball.

"Try hiding this under your tongue." She opened his jaws and thrust the pill in, clamping back his lower jaw. "Now swallow, you old bastard."

His eyes popped, but a massive involuntary gulp took place.

"That's better," said the sister. "I'm going off duty now. If I get a single adverse report on you tomorrow,

Plan A goes into operation. And that's only Plan *A*. Goodnight, Mr. Quy."

"You saboteur! You—you miscegenated daughter of a Limehouse pox-doctor. You—"

But his invective was addressed to a blank door and already his old lids were heavy.

He woke to a gentle but persistent shaking of his good shoulder. It was the redheaded nurse. He tried to sit up, but winced in pain.

"What time is it?" The day was bright outside the window.

"Eleven o'clock."

"Gawd, has there been a revolution in the hospital world? I thought your day started in the middle of the night."

"Sister's special orders, Mr. Quy."

"Don't mention that crab-faced hag to me."

"We're forbidden to hear blasphemy against sisters and matrons. Even when *we* do the blaspheming. Sister's all right. She's got a heart of gold, really."

"Brass, you mean."

"Anyway, Mr. Quy, I didn't wake you up to discuss Sister. You've got a visitor. Shall I send him in, or is there anything you want first?"

"Like what?"

"Like the bedpan, for instance."

"You're the essence of tact. I'll decline your generous offer. Send him in."

She ushered in a tall, fair-haired boy before departing.

The boy's eyes followed her. He turned back, grinning.

"They're looking after you, then, AQ. Can I put my name down?"

"You keep your mind on your studies," the old man said. "How are you, Alan, my boy? Come and sit down on the bed."

"You're stealing my lines. How are *you*?"

31

"Fine. Just a small failure of a minor strut. It's a self-repairing mechanism." He glared sharply at the boy. "Shouldn't you be at school?"

"I took the day off. Couldn't let an opportunity like this slip by. Almost as good as a grandmother's funeral."

"That's no excuse. You must keep up with your classes."

"Father says you never cared at all whether he attended school or not."

"Did he now?"

"Well, he implied it. Part of the speech when I get bad marks, about how much better opportunities I've got than he ever had, and all that jazz."

"We-ell, maybe I didn't care much. I was probably a bastard of an old man to him. But I couldn't help it." He sighed. "I always had a system of priorities that most people wouldn't agree with. And top of the list was my work. When I wasn't working, I was dreaming—which is probably the most important kind of work of all. I've gone through my life on dreams and hunches. I couldn't analyze things, in a laboratory or in myself. If you analyze things you break them down. Build, boy, build, that's what you've got to do. My hunch about your father told me that I'd pupped a conformist. There's nothing wrong with that. The world's full of conformists. If it weren't, there wouldn't be anybody to support people like me.

"I'm blathering on, boy. And misleading you. Of course you've got to analyze, separate the strands of a problem. But you've got to be ready to weave them together again in a new pattern. Creative analysis?—no, that's not the right word. To hell with it. You just obey your father. He hasn't done badly for himself. Nor for his family. You haven't reached the age of making decisions yet—not the ones that matter. I know he thought I never went to school. I didn't, more often than I could help—but I was reading, testing things all the time. I didn't get the chance of a university, or even a grammar school. If I had, I should probably have grabbed at them with both hands." He sighed again, more heavily.

32

Then he chuckled. "But, on balance, I'm glad I didn't get the chance. I wouldn't have got to where I have today.

"And where am I today? A bloody old wreck, a failure, lying in a hospital bed. Is that where? Not on your life, son. I'm on the threshold of something big at last."

"Are you, grand-dad? I knew it! As soon as—"

"*Grand-dad!*" the old man shrieked. "How many times do I have to tell you—"

The boy bit his lip. "Sorry, AQ, I forgot in my excitement. When they told me you'd blown yourself up, I knew that you must have been doing something way out."

"*Hrrmph.* Equating violence with importance isn't worthy of you. But we'll let that pass. This *was* violent. And it *is* important. The only snag is—I don't know yet just what it is I've stumbled on."

"You don't stumble on anything, AQ."

"Schmooze will get you nowhere. But, there again, you're right. *Nobod*y stumbles on anything. You've got to be looking, even if you don't know what you're looking for." His watery old eyes lost focus, and remained so for a full minute. They snapped back startlingly. "What do you know about superconductivity?"

"Er—it takes place when metals are cooled to absolute zero. Isn't that right?"

"Well, partly right."

"Is that what you've been working on? I bet that's a marvelous plant, isn't it? Just how do you get down as low as that?"

"Hold on! Who said I've been working on low temperatures? That was the whole point of the work. And it wasn't on metals. But since that was how superconductivity was discovered, and metals are the only substances it's been induced in up to now, let me give you a brief history.

"It started about sixty years ago when a Dutchman called Onnes liquefied helium—the only gas nobody had succeeded in liquefying up to then. And you're wrong about absolute zero. Kelvin maintained that at absolute zero metals would become perfect insulators, not super-conductors, because their electrons, instead of being movable without friction—which is what happens in superC—would become welded to their atoms and be immovable. Since nobody's got to absolute zero yet, nobody's proved it or disproved it. It's irrelevant to our main point, anyway, except that it's typical of the speculations that people came up with. They discovered all kinds of odd effects down there—and they got so bloody wrapped up in it that they didn't start wondering about whether superC could happen at more normal temperatures.

"At least, not for years, until about twenty years ago, when a scientist called Fritz London fancied that the same subatomic setup which occurred at very low temperatures might be discovered in large organic molecules like protein. Unfortunately London died before he had a chance to do much practical work on the idea. Then a Dr. Little of Stanford University picked it up several years later. He actually hypothesized the shape the super-conducting molecule would have to be—a long chain of carbon atoms which he called a spine, with alternating single and double bonds along it, projecting from which would be molecules of diethyl-cyanine iodide, which is highly polarizable and—"

"AQ—"

"—therefore capable of transmitting electrons freely—" He shifted testily. "Yes, boy, what is it?"

"You're leaving me behind, AQ. Diethyl-cyanide what was it?"

"Cya*nine* iodide. It's a dye used to sensitize photographic emulsions. Sorry, lad, I'm using you to go back over the steps I followed to see if I could get a clue. The real point is that Little's hypothetical molecule was ferociously complex, like the genetic molecule DNA, only more so. It meant engineering a molecule to specification—a molecule that, unlike DNA, doesn't exist in nature.

"Briefly, I thought I could simplify the specification.

34

Still complex, but attainable. I sold the research program to an electronics firm. Thirty years ago you couldn't have sold any organic chemistry idea to those lads—except maybe a new plastic for an insulator. But since Philips in Australia bred living crystals for transistor work, it's easier. I chose too small an outfit, that was the trouble, blast them."

"Why didn't you try the big firms, then?"

His grandfather broke into a fit of coughing. When it subsided he said, "Where was I? Ah yes. The commercial possibilities of superconductors at ordinary temperatures are enormous. A completely lossless conductor. Even for power lines, just carrying brute electricity, it would be a tremendous step forward, as you'd appreciate if you've ever tried to run a two-horsepower motor on too long a lead. But in the really subtle fields, in cybernetics, plasma physics, it would revolutionize them. Apart from what it might open up in organic cell structure itself, but we won't go into that.

"I cooked up various molecules and got various working samples. There's only a handful of firms in this country—in the world—equipped for that kind of work, but I commissioned a pretty fair outfit. Only the working samples didn't work. There's one thing about this field, if you've got it you've got it, and if you haven't you know soon enough. Like catalysts. The failures don't even yield much information. It's just a matter of altering the structure slightly and starting again.

"And finally I got it—or as near as dammit got it. Only I got carried away a bit. I was so cocksure that I gave it the works. The next I knew I was in here.

"But work this out. I put fifty thousand volts through a wafer of that stuff before it gave way. And it didn't give way in any ordinary fashion. Maddox, the manager of the company, was in to see me yesterday and I've got him believing that it was a buildup of the charge I gave the strip that was responsible for what was evidently one hell of an explosion. When he's had time to

35

think about it, if he can bring himself to it, he'll realize as well as I do that it couldn't have been.

"For one thing, you can *induce* a current in a closed superC circuit and it *will* build up, because there's no power loss. But this was direct transmission in a hookup. I had it loaded with enough impedance—the circuit, I mean, but the power was going through that strip, and it was acting perfectly as a superconductor—until I stepped the power up. Then it happened.

"On the other hand, it couldn't be a chemical reaction. Even if there was a chemical explosive potential in that strip, it wasn't big enough to shake the roof."

"Perhaps it was a combination of the two."

"Then it might have lifted the roof, but that's about all. Anyway, that molecule has got about as much ordinary chemical explosive potential as a lump of frog-spawn, pumped full of volts or not. No, the violence of that explosion was of a subatomic order. Atomically there would have been enough energy in that strip to have blown half of Belvedere Marshes off the map. But the setup was all wrong for that. Or was it? What have I discovered—a do-it-yourself low-power atom bomb? Not on your life. Do you know what I think?"

The boy shook his head.

"That molecule's organic—quasi-alive. I think I've somehow unlocked another dimension of energy—the energy inherent in life."

The boy's eyes widened.

"*Ach* no," the old man went on. "That's going back to Paracelsus and vital fluid."

He fell silent, staring into space.

"Enough," he said finally. "It's no good speculating in a vacuum. Not that I won't go on doing just that until they let me out of here. Then I've got to get back into Hypertronics. That's the first step. I'll make a last attempt to get them to let me carry on. For their own stupid sake. I can put millions into their laps if they'll only let me—and plenty enough for myself to investigate the other effect.

36

"But to hell with them and their job. The important thing is to get in there somehow and have a good look at the wreckage before some stupid bastard tidies it all up."

Five

Adolphe Quy stood before the gates. They weren't barricaded. They weren't as solid, even, as the ones that had been wrecked in the blast. They were wire over an angle-iron frame, a slightly more strutted segment of the rest of the temporary fence. But the guardian at the gates was as solid as he had always been. And the gates were closed.

"Hello, Fred," Quy said cheerfully.

"Oh, hello, Mr. Quy," said Fred, his big red face uncomfortable over his blue uniform collar. He took in the empty overcoat sleeve, the arm, still slung, beneath it. "How are you?"

"I'm fine, Fred. They let me out of hospital this morning." It was five days after the accident. The resident had finally given way, despite his voiced misgivings about the risk of complications at Quy's age. "I'll soon have this blasted sling off. Will you kindly tell Mr. Maddox that I'm here."

Fred, behind the wire, shifted as if his boots had suddenly got too tight.

"I'm sorry, Mr. Quy, I've got strict orders that you're not to be admitted."

"Well, just give him a buzz and tell him that I'd like to see him. Tell him—" he nodded to the suave, immaculately tailored, rather portly man by his side— "that I've got my lawyer with me."

37

"Well all right. But don't try any funny business, please, Mr. Quy."

"Funny business?"

Fred looked even more uncomfortable. "It's Mr. Maddox, Mr. Quy. He's like a man frightened of his own shadow. He comes down and briefs me every day, warning me to watch out for you. Some of the things he says about you aren't very nice at all."

"That's all right, Fred. If you'll just—"

Fred retreated to his hut, another temporary structure. Quy pretended not to notice that the gateman was keeping a wary eye on him and his companion as he spoke into the phone, but looked past the hut at what remained of the works beyond.

"Gawd, it is a bit of a mess, isn't it?" he said more to himself than to his companion.

The nearer end was a skeleton of new girders. The far end was shrouded in tarpaulins. An earth mover was gulping at the place where the stores had stood. The office block was latticed with scaffolding. The air was noisy with the clatter of cement mixers, the whine of lorries and other vehicles moving over the crowded landscape.

Fred came out of the hut. "Mr. Maddox says he'll be right down."

"Thank you, Fred. How's Charlie, by the way? It was Charlie who was on duty that night, wasn't it?"

"Charlie's no longer with us, Mr. Quy."

"Oh dear. I hope that wasn't on my account."

"Well, only indirectly, you might say. They've got round-the-clock gangs working on the rebuilding. The contractors have got their own night watchman. Union rules, or something. So Charlie was redundant. He was offered a job working on the rebuilding. The management has kept on all the workers. There's enough work, Gawd knows, sorting out this lot. A few of them, mostly skilled men, left. So did Charlie. Only he wasn't skilled, by any stretch of the imagination. Reckoned he had some kind of weakness in the back."

"I'm sorry to hear that. But—"

He broke off at sight of Maddox's square figure picking its way between the concrete-mixers and the lorries. He was puffing somewhat as he approached the gate and set himself firmly before it.

"Well, Quy?"

"I received your letter, tearing up my contract with Hypertronics."

"Determining it forthwith. I know. It was sent registered."

"You gave similar grounds to those you mentioned at the hospital last Sunday. I thought you might have seen reason since then."

"If you mean that I or the company might have changed our minds, the answer's no."

"Very well, before I bring suit against you for—"

"Please," said the character by his side. "Let me handle this." He spoke to Maddox. "My name is Goodman. I'm Mr. Adolphe Quy's legal representative. He doesn't mean *before* he files suit, but to safeguard himself in the event of any action. But I'm sure we can settle this without going to arbitration. He is merely stating his right to know the extent of the alleged damage."

"*Alleged*! Look around you. The contractors will be able to render a very accurate bill for the extent of the damage. If you want to go ahead and dispute them, the burden of proof would be on you."

"Not at all, I'm afraid, sir," Mr. Goodman said smoothly. "The contract, dated 19th September 1972, is the immediate *res disputandum*. Your primary grounds for setting it aside are that my client committed willful damage. If it were established that you or the company or any agent thereof in any way concealed the true facts from my client, I'm afraid that things would be prejudiced against you. *A priori* grounds of concealment. Mr. Quy doesn't wish to compound any alleged malfeasance. All he wants to do is look at the damage."

"He's looking at it right now."

"But the alleged willful damage is alleged to have

been generated in, at, and about a specific building, named in your letter as Special Research Building A. Can you see that building from here, Mr. Quy? Or any part thereof?"

"It's on the other side of the main building," Quy told him.

"You mean it *was*," Maddox said, impotent savagery in his voice.

"I do trust you haven't sought to remove any of the evidence already?" Goodman said suavely.

"Wait here," Maddox said. He turned on his heel and strode to the hut. Quy could see him lift the phone and speak into it. He spoke at some length. It was several minutes before he came out again.

"All right, Quy. I've been on to our lawyers. You can have ten minutes to inspect what's left of your research building. Under supervision. And it'll be my supervision. Fred, get young Chalmers on the gate and you come along with us."

There was a slight wait for Fred's stand-in to appear, then they duly made their way round to the back of the ruined main building, picking their way over duckboards.

"Strewth," Quy exclaimed when he saw the remains of the workshop. "You weren't exaggerating, Maddox."

"And we've got photographs to prove that this was the state of the place immediately after the incident."

"I'm relieved to hear that," Quy said, in all sincerity. Maddox looked at him warily, and kept close to him as he stepped onto the concrete floor. It was bare and hardly marked, except for where four bolts had obviously been wrenched violently out of it. Quy recognised them as the sockets where the stanchions of his main bench had been bedded.

"Well, there's not much left to inspect," Quy said. He walked over to the pitted remains of the walls, bent down and peered at them. He took a screwdiver from a pocket of his ragged overcoat.

"Wait!" said Maddox. "I said inspect, not tamper."

"Oh lord, Maddox, anybody would think they were made of priceless marble. They're not much use to anybody now. Another hole won't hurt them. But if you're worried that I'm trying to conceal anything, or plant it, all you have to do is watch closely."

He ferreted in the brickwork without further protest, then held up a tiny scrap of metal. "That's all I was winkling out. It's a bit of copper off the rig. Just establishing that it *was* my rig that blew up."

"Did you have any doubt that it was?"

"I've had no previous evidence. Don't forget that I don't have any direct knowledge of the accident at all. The first I knew about it was when I woke up in hospital and I was told."

"Well, are you satisfied now?"

"I suppose so. No, wait just a minute." He squatted down again. His eyebrows rose involuntarily. "No blue!" he muttered.

Maddox was standing by his elbow. "What did you say?"

"Nothing important." He made an entire circuit of the brickwork, half-stooping as he went, looking like a bad imitation of Groucho Marx. Maddox followed close behind him, so close that when Quy stopped suddenly and straightened he almost ran into him.

"That'll be all, Maddox," the old man said. "Thank you for your courtesy."

Safely outside, old Quy chuckled hugely. "Come on, Sid, I'll buy you a drink."

Over a scotch at the nearest pub, Goodman said, "Well, did you find what you were looking for?"

"I don't know. I don't even know what I was looking for. Let's say that now I start looking for what I found."

"You're a dark horse all right, Mr. Quy," Goodman said, shaking his head.

"And so are you, Sid. Where did you get that fine flow of legal phraseology?"

"Off TV. I hope I got it right."

41

"Don't ask me. But it sounded very authentic. You should have made it your career."

Sid glowed. "Do you really think so?" He sighed. "But it's too late now. You know how it is, you get a wife and family to support. Maybe you have big dreams, but you have to put them to one side. You build up a business. You hope it'll build up to be a big business, so you can retire early and do what you really want to do. By the time you find out that it'll never be a big business you're trapped, it's too late to change. You'll never be Goodman's of Park Lane and Fifth Avenue, but just the twelve-quid tailor down the Cally." He shrugged. "But you got to be philosophical. If I'd built up a big business, I probably wouldn't have been satisfied. I'd have wanted a bigger one."

"Everything's relative," Quy agreed.

"You can say that again. It's best to settle for what you got. You can still be Clarence Darrow or Alekhine in your dreams. Talking of Alekhine, Mr. Quy, when are you coming round for a game of chess again?"

"Just as soon as I get this problem licked. Life's pretty complicated at the moment."

Sid downed his drink.

"Have another," Quy said.

Sid looked at his watch. "No, there's just time to catch the twelve forty-five. I may be only the twelve-quid tailor down the Cally, but I can't afford to be away too long. Such a *dumkopf*, my Bernie. Are you coming?"

"No, I've got a few things to clear up down here first." Sid turned to go. "But you're forgetting something." Quy reached into the folds of his coat with his one good hand.

"What, the five quid? Keep it, Mr. Quy. Business ain't that bad. It was worth it, every minute of it."

Six

There was a *rat-a-tat* on the rickety door, and Alan burst in breathlessly.

"I came as soon as I could."

His grandfather looked at him amusedly. "What, did you run all the way?"

"I came by bike."

"Well, bring it in. What have I told you before? There's room in the scullery. People round here would do anything for you, but they've got a certain—ah—communal view of property."

Alan dutifully went out and wheeled his bike in, then rejoined his grandfather.

"Take a seat, son."

Alan picked his way through the clutter in the dimly lit basement room, found a clear spot on a divan and sat down.

Quy squinted at a battered alarm clock. "Five o'clock. You didn't cut any classes today, then."

"Couldn't—worse luck. It's our mock O-Levels this week."

"If I'd known that I wouldn't have rung you this morning. You ought to be indoors doing some last-minute swotting."

"Tomorrow's math. That's one subject I *can* skate. Wish I found all the rest as easy. Funny, isn't it, you can learn one subject easily, but another one seems so blooming hard. Especially when the ones you find hard are just a lot of facts, whereas—well, math, for instance, you've got to *understand* that."

"It's a question of what you want to understand. Feeling in your bones that there's some *purpose* in understanding."

"You don't believe in gifts, then—that somebody has a certain talent for a particular subject?"

"Nope. Well—I don't know. One thing I could never master was music. Your grandmother was a good pianist. I bought her a grand piano once. Once I tried to learn myself. I thought that it couldn't be too difficult, especially if you brought a bit of scientific method to it. But the scientific method got in the way. The books I read talked about minor chords and F Majors, but I wanted to know how many vibrations a second and how some discords could be pleasant to the ear. Like the one at the beginning of the slow movement of the Moonlight Sonata. I plugged away, in between times, for weeks. The cure came when I went into a pub and there was a fellow playing away like bloody Paderewski, and when I went over and bought him a beer I found he was a moron.

"That taught me something—something more, I mean, than the fact that I would never make a pianist or even a tin whistle player. That man was a moron only by the standards of the education peddlers. He'd accepted that role because that was the way he had been graded from the time they first started to try to teach him to read and write. He was probably illiterate. But a kid, when he starts school, has got to accept certain concepts that are jammed down his throat—that a vertical stroke with two arms sticking out of it is in some way the noise you make when you try and expel air from your mouth with your top teeth on your bottom lip.

"So the good little boys do as their teacher tells them, jump through the hoop and get labeled bright. But how about the kid who says to hell with this junk, first they've got to show me *why*? Of course, no kid is quite so self-aware as that, but it's an attitude. What happens to him? He probably winds up doing something he *can* see some sense in, like that chap at the piano. There was a man in America, didn't learn to read until he was eleven—or even speak much. Then—he must have come to terms with the setup. He finished up a doctor and a writer. His name was David Keller. That was a man of talent. But take a genius, Einstein. He wasn't exactly bright at school, either."

"But, if you mean there are no morons, how do you allow for geniuses?"

"I didn't say there weren't morons. Of course there are. You can't teach a Mongolian idiot calculus. And there *are* a few people, a very few, who refuse so flatly to imbibe the ideas that are spoon-fed to them, who are so determined to impose their own ideas, that *they* mould the world, not the world them. And I don't mean your bloody Napoleons or even your Lenins; I mean your Einsteins and Newtons. Empires, systems, rise and fall. All right, knowledge gets lost too, usually because of your world conquerors, but the geniuses change history once and for all, they change the way men look at the world.

"And that doesn't have to be a First Law of Motion or a General Theory of Relativity, anything as big as that. The first man who decided to weigh things changed science more than either of them. If the Greeks had weighed things, simple things like something before and after it was burned, we'd have had all the science we've got today two thousand years earlier. Or would we? That was *their* way of approaching the universe, that you only had to observe and deduce and you could find all the answers. They did pretty well, too, just doing that. And that's what your talent, or your gift, boils down to. The gift, if somebody develops it, is only the outward sign, pressured and distorted, of the world view inside. A man's personal coming-to-terms. What he decides he *wants,* what he *needs*—often for his own sanity's sake."

"Point taken. But I don't *want* French, for instance. And when—if and when—I pass O-Levels I won't have to. Trouble is, you've *got* to take it."

"I know, son, it's easy for me to talk. At your stage it's all compulsions. But nothing's wasted. I remember learning Russian once because there was some stuff that hadn't been translated that I needed desperately—or thought I did. Language is the root of this world view business. Every language has got concepts, words, that can't be expressed properly in others. The language itself is a world view agreed on by a tribe. *Ach,* but I'm blathering on, boy. And I didn't get you here to talk about language. I just thought you'd like to know that I've sorted out that other matter."

"You mean—the explosion?"

The old man nodded. "At least, I'm ninety-nine percent sure, and that's good enough for me. I was never one of your hundred percent merchants. But let's have a cup of tea first. The old mouth's dry. I'd just brewed up when you came."

Alan gulped. "I—I'm not thirsty, thank you, AQ."

"Nonsense, boy. Don't think I've got to the stage of ignoring the social graces completely. Five o'clock tea, and all that. Now, where did I put that other cup?" He rummaged among the clutter on the bench. "Ah, here it is."

It looked suspiciously grimy.

"No, really, AQ," Alan made a last attempt. But the old man seemed not to hear him. He poured a murky liquid from a blackened can that was standing on a tripod over a Bunsen burner. "It's already milked and sugared."

The boy took it, but when his grandfather turned to get his own and sit down, he put it down on the bare boards between his feet.

"Now," said Adolphe Quy, settling himself, "Are you ready?"

The boy nodded.

"Right, then." He paused eloquently. "The Meissner Effect."

"You mean—the insulating effect of a superconductor on a magnetic field?"

The old man's mouth fell open. "You mean—you knew all along? Why the hell didn't you say so that day in the hospital?"

46

"I—I'm sorry. I didn't know then. I've been reading up on the subject since."

"Have you?" The old man grunted. "You needn't sound so apologetic. I knew all about the Meissner Effect, anyway. I just didn't connect it with what happened. Gawd, there I was, lying in a hospital bed, with nothing else to do but think it out. And it was right under my nose. And I'll prove it to you. *You* could have reasoned it out if you'd known of the Meissner Effect then. *Reason*! Human blindness, makes a mockery of the word. Let me give you a brief and simple catechism just to show you. Ready? Right."

"What is the Meissner Effect?"

The boy looked puzzled. "You mean you want me to define it some other way?"

"Of course not! This is a catechism. I ask the questions, you answer 'em. Right, we'll start again. What is the Meissner Effect?"

"The—the insulating effect of a superconductor on a magnetic field."

"And what class of substances exhibit magnetic properties?"

"Class? Why, metals."

"And what class of substances did Kamerlingh Onnes find exhibited the phenomenon of superconductivity?"

"Metals, again."

"And what substance was I experimenting on when the explosion happened?"

"I'm not quite sure, AQ. Something like DNA, you said. Organic, anyway."

"Good. Metallic?"

"No-o. Not from what you said."

"Right, then. Now we're coming to the crux of it. Might we expect to find the Meissner Effect associated with these non-metallic superconductors?"

"I—I don't know."

"Come on, a grandson of mine can do better than that. Have a guess."

"Well—maybe. Kind of."

47

"*Kind of*! What a gloriously unscientific word. But all right. Kind of *what*?"

"Why—a kind of Meissner Effect."

"Exactly. Now then, just put those facts together in two parallel chains. Metal—magnetism—metal—superC —Meissner Effect. Non-metal—question mark—non-metal—superC—X Effect. X Effect being what I recently came out of hospital, from getting a sideswipe of, and apart from that scrap of knowledge we can't go much forrarder in substitution. But what was the other blank in that second chain?"

"Wait a minute. An equivalent of magnetism?"

"*I'm* asking the questions. How many more times do I have to tell you? You're giving the answers."

"All right—the equivalent of magnetism."

"And what is magnetism? Basically, that is. What kind of *thing* is it?"

"A force."

"All right. Now, what kind of force do we know of that resembles magnetism, but which affects other elements than metals . . . every other—"

"Stop, grand-dad. Let me finish it." The boy's eyes were wide now. And the old man's were bright.

"*Gravity*," the boy breathed.

"Gravity. The enemy. I was talking just now about weighing things. For that one job it was a precious ally, the Earth's gravity a yardstick. But in every other aspect it's been the enemy. Weighting our feet, an interference factor in everything man's ever tried."

The boy leaped to his feet.

"*Cavorite!*"

He laughed almost hysterically and went prancing round the dingy room, as if some minor power of anti-gravity had been generated by just discussing it, lifting his feet over and around the battered trunks, the scattered pullovers, the bits of machinery, in their path.

He stopped suddenly as he realized that his grandfather wasn't joining in, but just sitting looking at him with a pained expression on his face.

"What did I say?" the boy asked falteringly.

"Cavorite."

"Well? You know, H. G. Wells's substance in *The First Men In the Moon.*"

"I know, all right," the old man said testily. Then his voice and his manner softened. "Sorry, son. It wasn't your fault. The word brought back an unpleasant memory, that's all."

"Why? It was a pretty good book. I know it seems old-fashioned these days, now we've got rockets and bases on the moon, but—"

"It's not the book. It was your father. It must have been about '54 or '55. Not long before he married your mother. He had just got his Ph.D. and he came to see me. I was laid up at the time, so I hadn't been doing much active work. But I'd been reading the more, and thinking. And I'd come to the conclusion that there were two problems next on the agenda for man to lick. One was synthesizing life cells, the other was anti-gravity. It was only a few years then since man had learned to tap energy at will—atomic energy. It seemed to me somehow wrong that he hadn't learned yet to transform energy directly into motion, without having to *push* against something. Which is not only the crudest way of getting about—it's what a kid does the first time he climbs out of his cradle—but the *only* way man had found.

"I've got to confess that I didn't have any clear ideas on the subject myself then. I saw it as a matter of somehow being able to apply energy to iron out the wrinkle in space-time which is what gravity is. But here comes my lad, all bright and shining from college with his Ph.D. under his belt, and I ask him what's new in the physics world, seeing if I could get any hint of something I could link this anti-gravity chain of thought on to. But all he could talk about was quantum physics. So I came out with it and said, 'How about anti-gravity?' He just looked at me for a couple of seconds, and then said, 'What, Cavorite, you mean?' "

49

The boy looked puzzled. "But why should that be anything to—"

"Take umbrage at? Because I knew what he meant, and he knew that I knew. Find yourself a plate of material that happens to be anti-gravitic and you've got a perpetual motion machine. And perpetual motion is one of the phrases that's anathema to the hidebound, blinkered scientist. It's the 'perpetual' that sticks in their gizzard, and they swallow 'infinity' and 'zero' as glibly as you like. Your father was right of course. A perpetual motion machine is one that generates as much energy as is fed into it, despite what it uses and loses. And an anti-gravity screen, just like that, would generate a whole sight *more* energy—as much as you liked. Interpose the screen, up you'd go; take it away, down you come with all the energy of your fall. Just like a perpetual spring. I give your father credit; his mind was fresh enough—then—to see what inherent anti-gravity would mean. I just didn't like the way he regarded me—as some old idiot in search of some mythological philosopher's stone. The incorrigible in pursuit of the impossible, as I overheard him referring to me at a party once."

He broke off, looking apologetic. "I'm an old bastard, son, carrying on like this to you about your father. You ought to dot me on the nose."

The boy grinned.

"But let's get back to this special Meissner Effect," the old man said.

"Not the special Meissner Effect. Why not the ordinary Quy Effect."

"The Quy Effect! Why not, indeed? The *Quy Effect*. Sounds good."

"Are you sure you're right, though, AQ? I mean, have you got any confirming evidence?"

"A bit. All very simple and mundane, but it adds up to conducing proof in my book. First, let's get a clear picture of what happened. I had a workbench about ten feet long. On that I had, bolted, a pretty heavy testbed, a hundredweight or two. In that were two heavy terminals.

50

Between them was clamped my strip of test material. The terminals were connected, via a transformer and a hefty impedance, to a generator. I fed a couple of hundred volts through the strip. It held, it registered zero impedance itself. And then I stepped the voltage up, a few more hundred. It still held. Then I really went mad and shoved fifty thousand through it. And then—

"Now just what happened? The energy I fed into that strip created a Meiss—a Quy Effect—screening off the strip from Earth's gravity. And everything above it. You can rule out the minor attractions of other objects around, although that may have had some effect on what happened to me. I was one of the objects around. Now, since the Earth's going round the sun at a speed of something like twenty miles a second, not to mention its speed of rotation, sidereal drift and a few other factors, and you'll realize that a body suddenly removed from that influence is going to move—in a roughly upward direction—bloody fast.

"And so did my test strip—testbed and all. And this is where the difference between Cavorite and this comes in, resolving any paradoxes like perpetual motion machines. You've got to feed energy in to get it out. It was the electrical energy which—"

"Hold on," Alan said. "You said yourself that there wasn't enough electrical energy to have caused the explosion."

"I know. But it wasn't just the electrical energy. It was the whole force of null-gravity for a split second, the whole gravitational force of the Earth being harnessed, not fought against. Like tacking against the wind."

"But—isn't that back to the perpetual motion machine again?"

"It depends upon how big or how small you regard your machine. The universe is a perpetual motion machine for all we know as yet. Most paradoxes have only got any meaning because they set limits about a situation. Like Achilles and the hare. Achilles has got a hundred yards start, but the hare can run twice as fast. Yet the hare

51

will never catch up because by the time he has covered the hundred yards, Achilles has covered fifty. When the hare has caught up the fifty, Achilles is still twenty-five ahead. And so on. Of course, the hare *does* catch up, precisely at the two hundred yard mark. You've just set the limits smaller and smaller. All you're saying is that the hare won't catch up within a certain time.

"The gravitational force of a body is *there*, inherent either in it or the distorted space about it. Any engine man has ever made has extracted energy from something. If you had told a medieval philosopher that you could apply a small amount of energy to a lump of matter— under the right conditions—and get enough out to demolish a city, he would have thought you crazy. Yet he knew of the chemical energy inherent in wood or oil. He just hadn't heard of atomics.

"But where were we? Yes, with my little strip suddenly taking off. The bolts anchoring the testbed to the bench must have been tougher than the ones holding the bench to the floor, because it didn't stop to get rid of the bench. Now, as soon as dammit after it took off, it lost contact with its power source. Even so, it had obviously got such a hell of a momentum that it just went on traveling. For a split second it had been insulated from a body moving at twenty miles a second, plus various other components which we won't bother with, considering that escape velocity—the speed necessary for a body to escape Earth's gravitational pull—is only seven.

"There's no knowing what happened to it finally. It may have gone into orbit. I'll have to check to see if any unidentified satellite has turned up lately. They keep a pretty close watch these days. It may have gone on and be on its way to Sirius by now. Most likely it burned itself up in a few seconds in the atmosphere, like a meteorite in reverse.

"But before it did that, or whatever it did, it shifted itself and a whole lot of atmosphere out of the way, causing an implosion. Note that, an *im*plosion. By all that's probable I should have been crushed to death. But you get some highly random effects near the center of any blast. So much happens so quickly. Tangential forces, layer effects. I got caught in between a few of those, evidently, and went into a parabolic curve over the marshes. It's the things that can't move quickly that take the full force.

"Anyway, there's not much left from that night, but the little that is points to no other direction but. That strip was a vivid blue color, but I couldn't find a trace of blue about, although I did find traces of copper from other apparatus in the place. The area under the bench was untouched. The concrete wasn't cracked."

"But if there had been such a terrific upward force, wouldn't there have been an equally massive reaction? Wouldn't that have cracked the floor?"

"That's the point. If it had been an ordinary force, yes—enough to have made a sizable hole in it. But this force is reactionless. This *is* movement without reaction against a material object. Newton's Third Law of Motion up the spout, in fact.

"Final point in favor came when I went for a drink in a pub nearby. I was just leaving when I noticed there was all new glass in the windows. It used to be that old-fashioned pub glass, all curlicues and the name of the brewers in fat letters, and now it was modern translucent. Luckily the barman didn't know me, because when I remarked on it, he said that they'd had to have it done after some nut had blown up one of the factories down the road, hadn't I heard about it, and wasn't it a funny thing that the windows had blown out, not in? Before I caught the train back I carried out a spot check at a few houses. Told 'em I was a borough public safety officer, whatever that might be. *Everybody's* windows blew out, not in. One old dear talked about a *whoosh*ing noise a split second before the bang. Want any more confirming details?"

"I'll take your word for it."

"Good, because I haven't got any more confirming details. But I've got enough. There's only one thing needed to do now."

"What's that?"

"To duplicate the experiment. With proper precautions of course, against what we—you—have provisionally called the Quy Effect. *Against?* What am I raving about. To *harness* it."

He got to his feet and started to pace the room.

"So plans must be laid. I'd be flogging a dead horse trying to get Hypertronics interested again. But somehow I must get another sample of the compound."

"You mean—that one little strip was all you had?"

"It was all trial stuff, son. No sense in making up big batches until I hit on the right specification. It would have been hellishly expensive. It's not like knocking up plastics, or making a simple alloy. You've got to stitch each atom onto a molecule, just like a blasted court dressmaker stitching the sequins onto a ballroom gown. And it comes just as expensive. You need a firm with computers, cat-cracking furnaces, a squad of highly skilled technicians. I've got the right specification now, but even so I reckon it'll cost about ten thousand to make just one strip the size of the one that made the bang."

The boy looked suddenly sad.

"But that means to build an antigrav ship would take millions of pounds for the stuff alone. Wouldn't it? Won't you have to have the whole ship screened with it?"

"Here we are—back with blasted Cavorite! How do you see it—as the skin round a sausage? Anyway, who's talking about spaceships? And forget the cost. It's like a prototype car or plane. It costs a lot at first because you have to make the chemical equivalent of jigs and templates. Afterwards you can tool up a specialist plant and mass produce. The materials are cheap enough.

"But that's not the immediate concern. We want ten thousand quid now—or work to that value. You can bet your life Hypertronics has put the black in for me at the firm that made the other batches. That doesn't leave a very wide field to choose from. But somewhere we'll get it done. Mm-mm, ten thousand quid. Right. We move into action."

He started to tunnel into one of the trunks, scattering

54

old clothes and papers all over the place. Alan watched him in amazement. His grandfather was a genius, of course, and eccentric—but could he have ten thousand pounds tucked away in that battered old trunk?

"Ah—got it," said the old man. He held up a grayish looking garment. "My best shirt. How's your hand at the washtub, son? My left shoulder's still stiff. You should find a bar of soap in the scullery. Now—" and he resumed rummaging through the trunk— "where's that blasted plastic collar?"

Seven

"I wish to order letterheadings for my agency," Quy told the printer loftily.

"Certainly, sir."

"And I don't want any inferior rubbish. There's one in your window I rather like the look of."

"Yes, indeed. Perhaps you'd like to point out which one."

Quy went out with him and stabbed a finger at the glass.

"Ah, yes, sir. You have excellent taste." They went back inside. "That's an engraved heading, which means we have to order a die. That costs from ten pounds upwards. Of course, it soon pays for itself in quantity. And the paper is best mold-made. Quarto, six pounds a thousand."

"A thousand? Who said anything about a thousand?"

"Oh well, of course, we make a reduction for quantity. Just how many did you have in mind?"

"About fifty."

"Fifty thousand?"

"No, fifty."

"Fifty!" The printer's dreams evaporated with his smile. "We don't quote for fifty. Our minimum is two hundred and fifty."

"Piracy, but, all right, I'll take two fifty. And this is only a beginning, you understand. Take that into account when you prepare your estimate."

"You'd better have the jobbing samples book." The printer flung a dog-eared folio across the counter. "And the prices are standard. Extra for color."

"I don't want color. Nothing garish, you understand. Right, I'll have this one." Quy squinted at it. "Seven A."

The printer sighed heavily. "Two pounds, seven and nine, including tax."

"That's a hostile price."

"There's another place round the corner if—"

Quy brushed aside his words. "The name is The Organic Research Agency."

The printer reached reluctantly for a pad. "And the address?"

Quy hesitated. He had been undecided between using his real address and the phone number of the callbox on the corner, or that of a swank block of flats in the West End. He had used the latter device before—a pound tip to a porter could be a good investment. Both had their disadvantages. Number Three Caledonian Passage, N.1. didn't sound very impressive, and even with a pane of glass removed from the callbox it wasn't always easy to hear the ring. The second way wasn't foolproof, either. The porter would be round the corner having a pint when the important call came. An ad he had come across in the *Exchange and Mart* settled the point. *West End Address & Phone. Letters Forwarded. Strictest Confidence. Only Seven and Six a Week. Reduction for Longer Periods.*

He fished the cutting from a pocket and said, "Five Nine Seven Park Lane, W.1."

The printer looked up and grunted. "Do you want them posted there?"

"I will call for them personally. Tomorrow."

"You'll be wasting your time. You can have them Friday."

On Friday Quy returned to his basement with the headings, got out an antiquated typewriter and started picking away at its keyboard.

Brason Biolaboratories Ltd.
Anglia House
Norwich
Dear Sirs—

He stopped, cursing, as three type bars jammed. He picked them apart, getting his fingers messy and smudging the paper. He turned to hunt for an eraser, then peered at the page. The *a* was almost worn out and the *s* was a full eighth of an inch low. He could straighten the *s* bar. And surely it wouldn't defeat human ingenuity to write a brief letter without using an *a*?

His fingers poised to essay a first draft, deciding that the sheet of paper was too grimy now to use for a good copy, anyway. But he was stymied at the beginning with *Dear. Honored* Sir? *Ach,* they'd think he was a bloody wog.

He got up and hunted in the larder. He came out with a bottle. He held it up to the light. It was a quarter full. He grunted, picked up a sheaf of the letterheadings in the other hand and went out into the yard. He mounted the tottering wooden steps and banged on the upstairs door, his knuckles dislodging a small shower of desiccated paint particles.

The door opened and a red beard lit up the gloom beyond.

"Oh, hallo, Mr. Quy. How's the Mastermind?"

"Sorely in need of aid, Norman. But I come bearing sustenance."

Norman noticed the bottle. "Come *in*."

He led the way up to a large room. It looked tidy compared with old Quy's below, but only because the stuff littered about the place was mainly of one constitutent—

paper. Magazines, tearsheets, clipped typescripts, were arrayed in a direct ratio of disorder to their distance from a rolltop desk and its attendant leather-covered swivel chair. The room was plentifully furnished with book-shelves, but they were crammed full and as many books again were piled in front of them and heaped on any con-venient surface.

"Get the glasses, Norman, and let us commune."

Norman smacked his lips at the slug of rum the old man poured him.

"You couldn't have turned up at a better moment, Mr. Quy. There's been a change of policy in Torso, my main source of bread these past two years. Earthly vil-lains are out for my Anthony Hard series. Some dim gropings for international brotherhood and all that jazz in the managing editor's breast. So out go even such carefully denationalised villains as my Eurasian mutant with poison fangs and my Devil Daughter of the Incas. From now on it's got to be monsters from outer space. And I'm stuck."

"I wondered why I didn't hear the merry sound of keys clacking."

"I've been scratching like mad, and all the monsters I've come up with have either been used twenty years ago, or totally lack any kind of reader identification—on either side. Poison fangs, that's something the morons I write for can understand; they've got their candidates lined up in their sado-masochistic fantasies—their bosses, their wives. But how can you identify with a malignant green slime? Got any ideas, for chrissake?"

"How about a creature that can change into any shape?"

Norman looked sad. "That's as old as the hills."

"Is it? Well, how about one that's got a ray or some-thing that turns all the men into queers and—"

"*Eh*? Try giving my editor that one!" He lowered his voice to a kind of falsetto bass, *"Torso For Men.* No, thanks for trying, Mr. Quy."

"Well, how about one that can make your hero think

it's a nice bit of crumpet, eh? Telepathic hallucination. When all the time it's got teeth three feet long."

Norman brightened. "That's more like it! That's probably been used, too, but it'll do for a start." He wheeled his chair round to the desk.

"Won't it keep for a few minutes?" Quy asked. "I want you to type a couple of letters for me."

"Well, all right. One good turn and all that."

"Here's the headings."

Norman took them. "Hm-mm, sounds an impressive outfit."

"I'm glad you think so. Let's hope the recipients agree. Ready? Right.

Brason Biolaboratories Ltd
Anglia House, Norwich
Dear Sirs,
    You have been selected by our European agency to receive our order for a new experimental molecule."

"What you'd call a big order," Norman commented ironically.

"It *is* a big order, Norman. You might even say a tall order. Where was I? Ah, yes.

    Our preliminary survey indicates that you have the necessary specialized equipment and personnel for this assignment.
    Our initial order will be for a prototype strip of approximately twenty grams. Successful completion and delivery of this prototype will be a predisposing factor in our awarding a production contract running into eight

—no, hold it, that's a bit too strong—make that

well into seven figures.
    A detailed specification will be sent you on re-

ceipt of your intimation that you can undertake this order. But, as a guide, I can inform you that the molecule is a complex one of alternating single and double bonds with side chain molecules in the cyanine range.

Needless to say, we expect this matter to be treated with—ah—the confidence commensurate with the stature of our two organizations.

Yes, I rather like that phrase. "Yours cordially"—no, better not be too cordial at this stage—"Yours faithfully" —leave a space for my signature—"Robert J. Hopkins, European Director."

Norman raised his head and coughed.

"If you'll just type out two more like that, Norman. Just substituting two other names and addresses I'll give you."

"Looks as if you're cooking up a new life-form on your own."

"Not quite, Norman. But I'll invite you to the christening. That's a promise."

Eight

Two weeks later Quy knew that he had failed.

Brason Biolaboratories sent a printed card, regretting that their capacity was booked until the end of 1974. Biotechnics Ltd., with a London office in Regent Street, had written a cautious letter.

Dear Mr. Hopkins,

We thank you for your enquiry of the fourteenth. We do have the equipment and technical staff for

such a program as you outline. However, we have
not heard of your company till now, nor does a preliminary check in the various yearbooks and direc-
tories yield any relevant information. Perhaps you
are newly based here, with parent companies in-
corporated abroad? Your early advice on this matter
will have our immediate and closest attention . . .

"Too bloody close and immediate, I bet," Quy muttered.
The third reply forwarded from the accommodation
address stated,

Come out from behind the beard, Quy. Confidence
commensurate with the stature of our two organizations, forsooth! I'd recognize that style anywhere,
without the fact that I know Harvey Maddox.

It was signed "David Beck, Technical Director." He
remembered the name vaguely from years back. An
image of a tall lad with red hair and a big grin came
back to him. Another sad example of what success did
to a man, he lamented. And then he read the postscript,
"But have a drink for old times' sake," and he turned
the envelope up and a couple of pound notes dropped
out, and he felt like crying.
"Goddam and blast people! Why can't they be bastards
all the way through! A man doesn't know where he is."
But he tucked the notes into his pocket and went out
to the pub.
The Swan is perched on the canal where it passes
under Caledonian Road. That's where the road bends,
too, and what with the iron bridge and all, the Swan is
squeezed into a narrow strip. When Quy had first seen
the place, he had thought it was just like a set piece, all
plaster and mouldings, left over from a silent screen set.
He had walked in, half expecting to step straight into the
canal. In fact, some long dead and unsung Victorian
architect had made a crafty use of the site. There was

even a private dining room upstairs, used mainly for wedding receptions of the locals.

Quy pushed open the door and went in. "Hello, George," he said gloomily to the landlord.

"Hello, Mr. Quy. Long time no see. How's things? Heard you had a bit of an accident or something."

"A nasty one. A good many years ago. I got born."

"Eh? Oh, yes. Hah! we all had that one. What'll it be? Have one with the house."

"Thank you, George, but my demands today are too gross and would abuse your kindness. Give me a double whisky."

"I see what you mean."

"And have one for yourself. The poverty is in the spirit rather than the pocket."

"I'll have a Guiness, then, thank you very much. The best of luck. There's a friend of yours in the other bar, by the way."

"I have no friends. I even hate myself."

"Well, he's a neighbor of yours, isn't he? Norman, the bearded bloke. Shall I tell him you're here?"

"Send him in. Tell him there's a wake starting."

Norman came through, bearing a half-empty jug. "Hello, Mr. Quy. Have a drink. Just sold that story. You know, the idea you gave me."

"No, this is my wake. Have a double whisky."

"Make it rum?"

"Make it whatever you will, my lad. Enjoy the brief hour of choice before old age and predestination take you in their iron grip."

"Gawd! That's the mood, is it? You'd better drink up quick and have one with me while there's still time."

"I will, lad. And thank you."

"What's up, Mr. Quy? Things can't be as bad as all that."

"Can't they? *Ach,* we deceive ourselves. The only thing that keeps the human race alive, both individually and collectively, is a massive gift for self-deception. If we once took a hard look in the face at reality we'd hand

our chips in on the spot. What am I, Norman? I'm nothing but a bloody old failure. That's all my life has been—one long grey failure, redeemed only by flashes of brief and traitorous hope. I've got the brand of failure stamped on my brow like the mark of Cain."

He lapsed into a brooding silence, broken only by the clapping of his empty glass on the counter, accompanied by a nod to George.

"And now, when I've at last got something big to offer the world, nobody wants to know! I could change the course of history, and history goes on its way like the blind blundering hippopotamus it's always been. I'm kidding myself. History can do without me. There's probably some Russian bloody genius or some Yank, all crew cut and glasses, working on it right now. With a billion roubles or dollars behind him. Or some grinning Chinaman. Damn clever these Chinese. And where's the spirit of England gone? Down the bloody drain."

"And the spirit of Scotland is dribbling down your chin," Norman remarked.

"Is it?" said Quy, wiping vaguely with his coat cuff. "My mother always told me not to talk while I was drinking." He let out a prodigious sigh. "Look at that old sod in the corner there, sinking his gums into a pint. He never dreamed of glory, Norman, you can see that. He never wrestled with the unseen like us."

"Did you say the obscene? That's me."

"Let him be a shining example to you," went on Quy, undiverted. "And let me be a terrible warning."

The man in the corner became aware of the attention. He looked up at Quy and glared.

"Hey, dad," Quy called. "Have a drink?"

"Dad your bloody self," the other old man growled. "And you can stuff your bloody drink. What are you, a bloody Conservative, or something?"

"That's fighting talk," hollered Quy. "Hold me back, Norman."

Norman did no such thing, having a job to stop spilling the drink in his hand for laughing.

63

"I said hold me back, before I do something desperate. I've been called many things in my time, but never 'a bloody Conservative.' " And then he started laughing, too.

He suddenly found a grey-bristled face thrust in his.

"Who you laughing at?" It was the old man from the corner. "You wanna come outside?"

"God bless you, I'm not laughing at *you*. I'm laughing at the whole bloody world. As for stepping outside, I'm afraid my hernia wouldn't allow it. But thanks for the compliment. You've lifted me from the abyss of depression. Please have a drink."

The party broke up at three o'clock in the afternoon, when the pub shut. Quy staggered home on Norman's shoulder. They parted at the steps. Quy went in to his basement and flopped down on the bed. He stirred once, muttered "Maggie," then fell into a stupor again.

When he awoke, the light was gray in the sky. He levered himself up and went to the door. A chill in the air communicated itself to his bones, but it was a little time, as he peered bleeringly out, before he realized that it was the chill of morning, not evening.

He went back, took the tea can and emptied the tea leaves down the lavatory. Then he filled it with water and put it on the Bunsen. At each movement the dull ache in his head gave a jab. But he felt better in his soul.

When the water came to the boil, he ladled Nescafé into it. He sat down, sipping the black liquid, both hands round the mug.

"Maggie," he muttered. "I swore I'd never go back to you without the prize in my hands. A man's got his pride, even me. But it'll have to be, Maggie. Beggars can't be choosers."

He drained the mug and started sorting out his clothes. The best shirt was still clean enough; he had worn it only to the printers the once. He wiped the plastic collar clean. He located studs and a quite handsome mauve tie. At the bottom of one trunk were a strangely new-looking pair of shoes.

But a suit—that was the problem. He found two jackets and a pair of trousers to match each. But one pair was frayed to the point of raggedness. The other pair was passable, but its jacket wasn't. It was double-breasted and its broad lapels were horribly wrinkled, beyond the powers of any iron to remedy. It was filthy too. He had a presentable overcoat, but he couldn't go around all the time today in an overcoat.

He dived among the trunks again and surfaced with a tin box. He shook the contents onto the bed. They were all pawn tickets. He found one bearing the legend *Suit*. But the address, in small type, was Manchester, and it had lapsed by ten years. He turned up another that was still barely redeemable. He squinted at the pawnbroker's name, and cursed. It was in Tooting. He couldn't even remember the place—nor the suit. It might be a dinner suit. No, he'd pawned that not long after the war in the West Country, hadn't he?

He'd have to take a chance. The day was young. He could get a tube direct to Tooting.

He got back two hours later, under his arm a brown paper parcel that smelled strongly of carbolic. His nose wrinkled as he unwrapped it. The suit, a brown one, was in good condition, but it would need fumigating. He took it out and hung it on the line in the yard. He left the door open, the neighborhood being what it was.

He came back and stropped a razor blade round the inside of a glass. His hands were still shaking after the drinks of the day before, but he achieved a decent shave. He donned the shirt and tie and went out to retrieve the suit.

Other predators had been. He glared upward. "Bloody pigeons." He used a rag to clean the jacket sleeve. The carbolic odor had faded but, in doing so, had unmasked a strong underlying odor of mothballs. He cursed again, but put the trousers on. He had shrunk somewhat since he had bought this suit, he thought ruefully, running his

65

hand round inside the waistband. But it wouldn't show too much under his jacket.

He was less pleased when he looked in the mirror to comb his hair. How long had it been since he had last seen Maggie? Fifteen years? Must be. Soon after her husband had died. Fifteen. That meant that she couldn't be much over fifty. Wealthy, smart. He had seen a picture of her in the papers only a year or two ago.

And he looked an old wreck.

He threw on a dingy mac and went to the chemist down the road.

He went in and made his request to the girl in the pink nylon overall behind the counter. She hid her mouth behind her hand before she asked, "What color, sir? Auburn, blonde, black?"

Which had it been? More of a cross between mouse and ginger, if he remembered.

"Chestnut?" the girl suggested.

"That'll do," he said.

"Five and six, sir. Be careful not to get it in your eyes when you apply it."

"D'you think it's for me?" He snatched it from her, flung coins on the counter and went back to his basement, quivering with indignation.

There he followed instructions and sat reading an ancient copy of the Times Engineering Review until it was dry. Then he went back to look at the result in the cracked mirror above the sink.

Fool! His eyebrows stared starkly white. He sploshed some of the dye on a rag and rubbed hard. That was better. They could dry en route. But the hair looked *too* dry. Like bloody rusty wire.

He found some Vaseline which he rubbed in. Then he combed and brushed it, whistling "When You and I Were Seventeen" between the gaps in his teeth. Subliminally prompted, he rummaged in the trunk, found a denture, rinsed it, and smacked it in his jaws. It was a bit loose, like the trousers, but it filled the gaps and plumped out his lean cheeks.

66

On with the coat, and it was done. He craned in the tiny mirror to get as much of the effect as possible, and was hugely pleased. But the smell of mothballs bothered him. He found a bottle of aftershave lotion that Alan had bought him one Christmas and sprinkled it liberally over his garments.

"Now, fight it out," he said blithely.

He passed out of the peeling door into the light of day. A series of ads from pre-war days came suddenly to his mind. For bath salts, hadn't it been? "Into the bathroom goes Aunt Aggie. Out comes Miss Agatha Anstruther, M.A., L.R.C.M. Lecturer in the Pianoforte." "In goes old has-been Quy," he murmured to himself as he proceeded down the alleyway, "Out steps Adolphe Quy, Esquire, M.B.E., Mover of the World," and did not notice the figure that brushed by him, until a bottle of milk clattered on the stones behind him.

He turned. It was Norman.

"Strewth!" said Norman. "It *is* you!"

"Who else? I trust that I did not occasion your small mishap?"

"Don't you worry, Mr. Quy. A very small price to pay."

At the station, Quy stopped to buy a carnation, and then a cigar at the kiosk. He rarely smoked, but Maggie always liked the smell of a cigar. And it suited his ebullient mood. On a sudden thought, he went into a call-box and consulted a directory. Maggie was still at the same address. He came out and hailed a taxi with lordly gesture.

"Three two five Clargies Street, Mayfair," he told the driver.

It was only when the taxi wheeled to deposit him outside the small discreet apartment building, that he felt his confidence ebb. Maggie would be out. She was a career woman, after all. It had all been for nothing.

His legs felt shaky as they ascended the steps, and worse as he stood in the lift that took him to the top floor. He got out and lingered in the thick-carpeted hall to light the cigar. Now he found himself praying that she

67

would be away. "*Ach,* Quy," he told himself, "You're acting like a love-sick schoolboy," and he rang the doorbell.

A pretty, foreign-looking maid answered the door.

"Lady Wentworth?"

"Who is calling, please?"

"Mr. Adolphe Quy."

"Just a moment, sir."

She retreated behind a chastely carved door on the other side of the hall. But it was Lady Wentworth herself who came out.

"Ado! How good to see you! Where have you been all these years?" She embraced him warmly.

"Hello, Maggie. You're looking fine."

She had never been of model slimness, and now she couldn't have been called anything but plump, despite the sleek silk dress and the doubtless expert foundation beneath it. But she was maturely handsome, one grey streak in her blonde hair.

"Come in." She showed him into a room that brought back memories to him. It hadn't changed that he could recollect. Then, with furniture like this, there could have been no need. Chippendale and antique carpets didn't need renewing every ten years. She ushered him to an armchair, and turned away. "Sophie, bring in the whisky."

She turned back to Quy.

"Mm-mm, you look pretty good yourself." Her nose had detected mothballs, but Ado had always had a faint aura of them about him when he was dressed up. And his hair. Memory might fade, like a snapshot, but not as quickly as that. Or reality faded quicker. He had already been greying when she had last seen him. He had probably forgotten that. How old was he, the old lamb? Getting on for seventy, surely.

"Thank you, Maggie. Things could have been worse. How about you?"

"You only have to read the financial pages. Then, they were never your favorite reading, were they?" She sighed.

"The struggles are all over now—have been for years Poor old Andrew, he did all the donkey work."

"Modest as ever!" Quy said chidingly "You know he wouldn't have got anywhere without you He knew what he was doing."

"What, when he picked me out of the office?"

"He had a few of the good years."

"All too few. And now—" She sighed again. "A company becomes a self-perpetuating machine. The danger of shipwreck gets more and more remote as the direction gets into more and more experienced hands. It spreads the chances. Of course, when a fair-sized company does hit the rocks, it hits 'em. Sometimes I think that the slim chance of that happening is all that keeps me from selling up and going to live in the Bahamas or somewhere. Still, that would be the most likely thing to upset the steering. It's still my money—or Andrew's—that's the core of the business. But I sometimes kid myself the few odd times I put a word in, that that word helps."

"You wouldn't want to start all over again, would you?"

She fingered her glass reflectively, then looked up with a faint smile. "No, I suppose not. It would be like having to start to walk again. And I got enough bumps the first time. Still, let's not get maudlin. What have you been doing, Ado? Still inventing, still pushing back the on tiers?"

"Trying to. Nothing very notable, I'm afraid. Until—until now."

"Now?" Her voice was suddenly cautious.

"I've made the strike, Maggie, at last. The great discovery. I'm out on my own this time, too—I think."

"I'm so pleased, Ado. What is it?"

"Anti-gravity."

She looked sad. "Oh—picking yourself up by your own bootstraps?"

"That's what it amounts, to, Maggie I know what you're thinking. It's in the category of perpetual motion

69

machines and eternal youth serums. But they're man's dreams. Dreams *can* come true."

"I'm disappointed in you, Ado."

"Why? For thinking I can conquer gravity? But I—"

"No," her voice was suddenly hard. "For taking me for an old ————"

"*Maggie!*" The word was coarse. It sounded horribly so on her lips.

"All right," she flared. "I didn't forget plain language when Andrew got his knighthood and I became Lady W. You've come here to try and take me for a few hundred. At least, don't insult my intelligence. I may have been bright only on the financial side of Wentworth Engineering, but I picked up quite a bit of technical know-how on the way."

Quy's hand holding his whisky glass trembled violently. Then the glass fell and his head was bent in his hands, his shoulders shaking.

"Ado, Oh, *Ado*." Then she was suddenly hardheaded again. "Look up, man. Look at me."

He lifted his head for a moment, then it slumped again. And there was no doubt about it. She had seen a man cry before, but Adolphe Quy was the last man she could have pictured.

"Sophie." The maid came running. "Bring Mr. Quy another glass."

She filled it nearly full and knelt down beside him.

"There, there, love. Drink this." She took his arm and it felt terribly skinny. Should she offer him lunch, she wondered. The poor old bastard probably hadn't eaten for days.

Quy waved his arm feebly. He lifted his head.

"Not just now. Sorry about that." He sat up. "I did come here for money. But don't doubt my word. I wouldn't lie to you, Maggie. I didn't last time. I *did* have an idea for a revolutionary new engine. I just didn't know that somebody else was developing the linear induction motor too."

"I know," she said gently. "You sent me the cutting."

70

He was reviving, but his voice was heavy with regrets. "We were going to call it the Maggie Wentworth, weren't we? I didn't know whether it was going to be a car or a train." He gulped. "I only got as far as a little trolley on wheels, Maggie, but it *worked*. And then I picked up a paper with the news that somebody had beaten me to it. I didn't want to come back like this. I'm not broke, Maggie. Not quite, anyway. I've been a bloody sight harder-up most of the time these past years than I am now. All right, I came here to put the finger on you. But for something, Maggie. For *something*."

"But for *what*? Why didn't you say what it is? Why try and sell me a gold brick?"

"I didn't. I'm not. It's what I said it was—antigravity. It's not a gold brick—except a real one. Look, won't you *please* believe me? I may be getting on a bit. Maybe I broke down. That's one of the complaints of age, like prostate trouble. Thank Gawd I don't suffer much from either of them. And I'm not going off my chump. I've never been sane enough to go crazy." He sniffed. "And, thank you, I will have that scotch."

She handed it to him. "And have another cigar. Yours seems to have expired in the ashtray."

"No, not the cigar. Not now. I don't really like them all that much. I only smoked it because you like a man to. The same as these clothes and all." He took a gulp of the scotch. "But I didn't put them on just to—I mean, I would have tried to make myself look as good as I could, coming to see you. If I *hadn't* wanted anything. I would have come to see you before, only after the last time—"

He broke off, and took another drink.

"Listen, Maggie. I won't go into a lot of technical detail. It's not engineering of your kind. Not like the linear motor. Do you know what a superconductor is?"

"Yes."

"You know what the Meissner Effect is?"

She shook her head.

"Well, it's simply the fact that a superconductor in ac-

71

tion is impervious to a magnetic field. I was working for a company, until a few weeks āgo, trying to develop an organic molecule that would behave like a superconductor at ordinary temperatures instead of only at near absolute zero. And I found one, only this non-metallic superconductor generated its own kind of Meissner Effect—it was impervious, not just to magnetism but to gravity."

"That seems to make sense. But you say you were working for a firm. Surely anybody could see the possibilities in this, if you could show it to them working? Why isn't the firm backing you?"

He coughed. "We-ell, there was a little matter of nobody being around when it happened. And I couldn't duplicate it because the blasted test strip just took off. Taking half the works with it."

"Wait a minute. Not Hypertronics?"

He nodded.

"Oh, no! I might have guessed. I was in Athens at the time. I read about it in the airmail *Telegraph*. I knew the name because they had supplied us with a few things from time to time. Well, I can understand why *they* won't finance you."

"You do? Do you know Maddox, their boss?"

"Maddox? Never met the man. But his company went into liquidation yesterday."

"I didn't know. I'm sorry."

She laughed, but it was half a sigh. "No, you're not, you thumping old hypocrite! All you care about is your own ideas."

"We-ell, I have to say I am. Sorry, I mean. Don't I? Actually, I'm a bit relieved. I wondered why I hadn't heard from them. They did talk of slapping an action on me for a million, besides charging me with false pretenses. Which could have been a nuisance."

"Why—*were* there false pretenses?"

"Honest to God, Maggie, no. I may have sold myself a bit strong to them. But *caveat emptor*. And I could have made a fortune for them—if only with the superconductor."

72

"What's the good of a superconductor that you can't hold down?"

"I don't think the Quy Effect—that's what my grandson Alan christened it—shows itself until you pump a certain voltage through it. But I'm not interested in holding it down. I want to get it off the ground."

She shook her head. "Ah, the Maggie Wentworth rides again, is that it? Or should it be flies? Or floats?"

"It will, Maggie. This time it will!" He stopped short, gnawing his lip. "But it's not just a matter of a few hundred pounds. This is a pretty expensive molecule to cook up."

"Could my firm help in the actual cooking?"

"Afraid not, Maggie. It's a different line of country from anything your people could handle. The prototype will take a bit of engineering, but elementary stuff that I can handle myself. It's the molecule that will take the money. Or a few million of them in one little piece."

"All right. Out with it."

"Ten thousand."

"*Ouch.*" She looked at him for a long time. He returned her gaze, trying to look every inch the dedicated and responsible pioneer. In fact, she thought as she looked at him, he looked like an apologetic child.

Then she sighed and went across to a Chinese Chippendale bureau. She came back with a checkbook and wrote quickly.

"Oh, make it cash, will you?" he asked anxiously. "I've still got a few creditors lurking about. They could make a hole in that if I put it in a bank and they got wind of it."

Nine

He was sitting in a glass room suspended over Regent Street, facing a scholarly-looking young man across a desk that shone dully bronze.

"I've brought the specification." He took out a long envelope and passed it across the desk.

The other opened it, scanned it for a time, then looked up.

"This is pretty complex, Mr. Quy, even for Biotechnics. I'm not sure that your suggested sum of ten thousand pounds will cover it."

"I don't see why not," Quy riposted. He had never bothered himself overmuch with the figures at Hypertronics, but he had a pretty shrewd idea of the cost. It was difficult, of course, to dissociate the cost of the preliminary work, the failures, from that of the one successful sample. The former had been by far the larger, but each successive sample had, with increased expertise, been easier to make. Each had involved only a slight shift—an atom or two—from the previous one. He himself had picked up some knowledge of the techniques. Which made it infuriating that he couldn't go back to the firm who had done the work then. But his surmise had been only too correct. A phone call had shown him to be as *persona non grata* there as he had been at his late employers.

"We've prepared a contract, in any case," the other went on. "I have it here. You'll see that we do not undertake to deliver an actual specimen, as long as we supply you with costed proof of work done."

"And who does the costing?"

"We will. I'm afraid you'll have to take our word for it. It works both ways; the contract provides for a refund if the specimen should be achieved at a price below the figure."

"Your costing again, I suppose."

The young man began to show slight signs of wearing patience. "It's a standard contract for this kind of work."

Old Quy squinted at him. "How about if I come in on the job myself?"

"I'm sorry," the young man said quickly. A trifle too quickly? Quy wondered. Things got around. Perhaps it had been a mistake to use his own name, carried away by the fact of having ten thousand quid behind him this time. "That wouldn't be possible. Of course, if at any time you wish to make a progress check, I can almost certainly arrange for a visit to our laboratories."

Quy glowered at him. It was difficult to make out the tone of these smooth characters who seemed to infest science these days. He sounded like a head waiter saying that he might be able to arrange a table. Did *he* expect some kind of a consideration too? He looked at the grey suit, the button-down collar, the button-down face above it, and decided to let that one go. There was a more disturbing point lurking in the words.

"At any time?" he barked. "Give me that contract." He peered at it, then looked up. "Except for the dotted line under the one for the signature, there's not a space for a date on this thing."

"It's an open-end contract. So we can't put in a completion date."

"It's open at both ends. Where's the starting date?"

"We can't commit ourselves to one. But let's say we pencil in—" he looked at a desk calendar which said May 24—"July ten?"

"July ten my backside. And let's say we do the writing in ink. I'll give you fourteen days to begin it. If you want the contract, that is." He started to get to his feet.

The young man stiffened. "Just a moment." He reached

for the phone, changed his mind and got up. "I'll be right back."

"Before you go haring off," Quy told him, "let me tell you that I don't go along with this open-end gobbledegook one little bit. There *is* a closed end to this. Ten thousand pounds." He cursed himself silently at the mistake in tactics. His brain couldn't be as agile as it used to be. He added quickly, "Not that there isn't plenty more after that, if necessary. Ah, when I go into production, that is. But this is all time-rates and overheads. You can get one of your costing clerks to turn up a figure on just how many days that'll add up to."

"It's not as simple as that," the other said. "But I'll see what I can do." In a slightly more genial tone, he added, "Make yourself at home while I'm gone."

Quy looked around him, wondering who could make himself at home in a glass house with metal fittings like this. A robot? But things were going well. He didn't kid himself for one minute that ten thousand pounds paid the overheads on this one office for many weeks. On the other hand, this was a new branch of the industry, and his a novel order. He picked up a copy of *Fortune* from a stainless steel magazine rack, and riffled through it while he waited. He stopped at a feature article, headlined "The Boom in the Rocket Industry" and chuckled. Well, that was one boom whose days were numbered.

The young man came back finally.

"It's settled. We can start clearing the ground for this and put a fixed starting date of July first in the contract."

"And delivery date?"

The young man coughed into the tips of his fingers. "We call it terminal cost date."

"Call it what you bloody well like."

"Terminal cost date," the other repeated, unperturbed, "August ten."

Quy frowned disgustedly, then heaved his shoulders. "All right."

"Fine, Mr. Quy." The other hesitated ever so briefly.

"We should, of course, require the full cash payment before we proceed."

Quy reached in his jacket pocket and flung down a bundle of notes on the desk. "Count those. I think you'll find two hundred fifties there."

The young man recoiled. "I didn't mean actual *cash*." But he brought himself to pick up the bundle. "I'll get you a receipt for this, get the dates typed in the contract and we can sign." He started to leave the room again, then turned.

"Oh, one small point. We had an enquiry in, a week or two ago, on very similar lines—engineering a molecule very much like this one. From an organization called Organic Research Bureau. You're not connected with them, are you?"

"Never heard of them," said Quy blandly.

He spent the intervening time in the backyard, rigging up a contraption that looked like a sled. It was about six feet long, something over two feet wide and made of heavy angle iron. He hired a welding kit from the garage up the road. From a government surplus store he got a petrol engine with a name on it that he recognized as makers of marine engines, an electric generator, Field Model Mark IV, and a transformer. It made a pretty clumsy power unit, but it would have to do.

He welded them into the top of the frame. Underneath it, a foot or so from the ground, he fixed a dural plate through which, heavily sheathed, two cables led from the generator to thick terminals. He walked around it for a day, then went back to the surplus store, got a walkie-talkie set, stripped it down and assembled a radio control unit out of it. He welded the receiving half of that, too, onto the frame and connected it up. And covered the lot with a tarpaulin. Finally, he staked the tarpaulin down, linked the stakes to a crude but effective alarm circuit and tucked the bell of the alarm under the stretched tarpaulin. The whole assembly was too weighty, and of too little value—except to him and his hopes—to be worth stealing, but he wasn't taking any chances.

And then he waited—for that was all there was to do.

He tried to get down to scraps of projects from the past, anything to keep his mind engaged, but it was no use. His mind kept returning to the suspended project in hand. He started to go to the public library every day, asking Norman to keep an ear cocked—for both the callbox phone and the burglar alarm.

Neither sounded. It was a long, yawning summer. By the end of July his patience was wearing thin, and he couldn't stand the sight of any more books. "The blasted human brain's like a bathtub," he grumbled, frustration squeezing heresy out of him. "If you add a gallon of facts from the tap, a gallon that's already there slops over down the overflow. What precious facts am I sending down the waste pipe?"

Sometime during that hot dry summer a brightly colored card came from Alan from Austria, and a week later one from Yugoslavia. Then, one morning at the beginning of August, the lad himself turned up, his legs brown in brief *lederhosen*, his face even browner under hair bleached almost white.

Old Quy was standing by the callbox at the end of the passageway—a favorite haunt of his these past few days. He was too startled at the apparition to notice the look of misery on the boy's face for a moment. Then it registered.

"What's up, son?"

"I got back from Europe last night to find my exam results waiting for me. I failed."

"Oh."

"I passed Math easily. I knew I would, I told you. And I got through Physics. But I failed English, French and Chemistry. Oh, I passed Geography. Lord knows how. And as if it mattered."

"You can take them again, can't you? What's a year at your age?"

"A bloody sight more than it is at yours!" the boy burst

out. Then he bit his lip. "Oh, I'm sorry, AQ, I didn't mean that."

"All right, son. I know what you mean. It isn't true, though. But come on—I've got something I want to show you."

He led the way into the yard and fumbled with the stakes. A shrill ringing started. "Well, the burglar alarm works all right, anyway," he said. He silenced it, then lifted up the tarpaulin.

The boy gaped at the contraption. Then his eyes went from one component to another. Finally, he squatted down and looked under the plate.

"It's the machine! That's where the strip of whaddyama-callit goes in, isn't it?"

"That's a bloody scientific name! Still, it hasn't got one yet, has it?"

"Quyite?" the boy essayed. "No, that hasn't got the right ring to it—not like The Quy Effect. We'll have to think of something. Wait a minute—you mean you've managed to get a sample made?"

"I've got one on order, boy. I'm expecting it any day now."

Alan looked at him sadly, suspiciously, remembering school stories that he had given up reading only a few years before. His grandfather wasn't exactly the build of Billy Bunter, but he was just as much the incurable optimist.

AQ got the message. "Honest, son. I raised the wind. As soon as the strip arrives we'll bolt it in and have the maiden flight."

"What—here?" The boy looked around him—at the little yard, the houses clustered round.

"Well, maybe we'd better choose a more isolated spot. The neighbors are too nice to risk what happened the last time happening again. But I think I've got it under control. We'll have to have somewhere where there's room for all the pressmen, too."

"Pressmen? You're going to show it to the world, then?"

"Of course. That's the whole idea."

79

"But isn't that—well—risky? Oughtn't you to get it patented first?"

"You can only patent an appliance—not just an idea. Until I get the strip I won't know whether this *will* work. I've got every confidence, of course, but I still don't know just what's going to happen when I switch on. Last time I was dead beat, after working pretty near continuously for several days. I'm not sure just how long I built up the current. I know I was jotting down the details, but my notes went up with everything else.

"But I tidied up the specification of the molecule. Not enough to alter its superC but enough to render it more stable—I hope. For all the computers and electron microscopes and general paraphernalia of molecular engineering, it's still a hit-and-miss matter. You've got to *feel* it, more than think it. I'd better qualify that. It's out in a region where intuition's as important as reason. Probably that's why I like this field so much, though I didn't know much about it before. My few months at Hypertronics were the happiest in my life. I only wish I could have a real go at this molecular tinkering—get right down there in the spaces between the atoms! Where was I? Oh yes.

"I'm hoping that this time the effect will show itself at a lower voltage level. I think . . . I *hope* . . . it'll build up gradually, *controllably*. It's all hope, I suppose. If it works I'll have no more difficulty raising money—all the money I need to develop it as a real practical means of locomotion. I'll have the bastards eating out of my hand yet. If it doesn't—"

He hunched his shoulders.

"It'll work, AQ. But you'll want proof. I'll bring my movie camera along."

"That's an idea, son. But I'll make sure there's proof, all right. The press, the TV boys, the newsreel companies, they'll all be there, you'll see. I'll send out proper invitations to all of 'em."

"Fine! We'll drink to it. Come on, I'll buy you a beer."

The old man squinted at him. "Beer now, is it?" He licked his lips. "I won't say I couldn't do with one at that."

In the Swan, having got two pints of bitter, Alan looked around him. "A bit different from Austria." He took a swig at his jug and pulled a face. "Bit different from their beer, too. The beer in Salzburg is the best in the world."

"You're an authority now, then?" his grandfather said sarcastically.

"Well, it's supposed to be. It's light and cold—and strong." He tried his best to look a man of the world, one young brown arm draped over the arm of his chair. "But it didn't have any effect on me. One of the lads in our party, though—"

"You watch it," his grandfather said roughly. "There are more important things in the world at your age than guzzling beer."

The boy's man-of-the-world air collapsed. His arm dropped and he sat hunched up in the chair, looking hopelessly in front of him.

"Why'd you have to remind me?"

"Sorry, son. Don't brood over it. You said a year's more important at your age than it is at mine. At least you can reckon on another year—unless you drink yourself to death."

The boy could only raise a feeble smile.

"How about me?" went on Quy. "I might peg out before I get anywhere with the Quy Effect. I might peg out tonight. Then there won't be any Quy Effect, because it hasn't happened as far as anyone knows. Just a handful of notes that won't mean a thing to anyone else, and a handful of decomposing brain cells."

"*Grand-dad!*" the boy looked shocked out of his depression now. "I've never heard you talk like that before. You mustn't."

"It's a fact." The old boy seemed to be luxuriating in the morbid speculation now. "And, in a few years' time, or a month's time, somebody else will discover it and it'll be known as the Petrov Effect or the Wang-Fu Field. And somewhere, rotting in the stainless steel vaults of Biotechnics Limited, will be a specification and a strip of stuff

81

that nobody came to collect and that nobody there will have the slightest clue to the use of."

He sighed a rumbling sigh.

Alan clapped his hands over his ears. *"Stop!"* A face looked up at the other end of the bar. More quietly, but insistently, "You mustn't talk like that."

The old boy grinned. "Well then, stop moaning about your own lot, boy. Self-pity is sterile. I suppose I've done my share of it at times—not without reason, probably—but to hell with it! I know competition's fierce at your age. But you can put next year to good use. Don't just look at it as making up lost ground, or getting the required mark, but getting a better understanding of the subject. A better base, a better springboard. Even if it *has* taken you a year longer."

The boy winced. "Dad said more or less the same thing —after he'd cooled down. But he was hopping mad. And disappointed. He wants me to join his department at the Ministry. It's his dream, I know."

"And not yours?"

"Some dream!" His voice was withering.

"Hey—don't lose all perspective."

"Well, what do *you* think about dad's work? It's all right, you don't have to tell me."

"It could be a good job for you. If you're good at Math. That was never *my* strong point."

The boy looked at him with an intensely puzzled expression on his face. "I know what you think of Ministries and government departments. And I know you don't get on with dad. But—how can you be against *his* work and yet recommend it for me?"

The old man took a swig of his beer before answering. And even then he didn't immediately.

"I probably couldn't answer that if I wanted to," he said finally. "I know I wasn't much of a father to *your* father. Maybe it's guilt. But I'm not going to make the same mistake twice. I'll give you advice—for what it's worth— but I'm not going against your father's wishes—at least, as far as you're concerned. Transference comes into this. *He*

82

wanted to follow in my footsteps. Perhaps that was why I was brusque with him, because I knew that my footsteps led through a lot of struggle and misery at times, and I wouldn't want my son to have to go through it all. Perhaps I realized that he wasn't as tough as me. I could do *that* for him, at least. Perhaps the poor b—" he stopped, and coughed—"perhaps he feels that it was somehow *his* fault. It wasn't. Anyway he wants to make it good in you. And I want to make it good, if I can, in you. Nobody's made the same, and there aren't many made the same way as me—thank God. So, if your father wants you to join him—join him, unless you've got something else in mind."

"I haven't—yet. Oh, it's so blasted difficult!"

"I know, son. But things will sort themselves out."

"It isn't working with the old man. It's—well—I'm against what he does. He's in weapons."

"I see. You're against weapons, then?"

"I'm against the kind of weapons we've got today. Isn't everyone?"

"Everyone's against death, too. We live in a complex world. So the weapons are bound to be complex."

"Complex?" The boy sneered. "Inhuman, you mean. It's not war any more. It's destruction. I'm not a pacifist—at least, I don't think I am. If somebody punches me on the nose, I'll punch 'em back, and bloody quick. War might have been honorable once, but it isn't now. Joining the old man's department would be as bad as putting a uniform on."

The old man sighed. It was almost to himself that he said, "The world *is* complex. So bloody complex that in one lifetime you've got to clear your own path and not be distracted."

"What—by human feelings? Is that what you mean? Principles, *everything?*"

"Oh, can it, son. Or I'll hit you on the nose right now. There's a pernickety strain in the Quy family. Have another drink." Quy got to his feet.

"I'll get them, AQ."

His grandfather wrenched his jug from him. "What, do you think I'm an old cripple, or something?"

When he got back from the bar, his grandson had got over his depression, at least for the time being.

"Cheers, AQ." He looked up from his beer and said, suddenly, "Why do you call yourself Kwye and my father pronounces it Key?"

"You call yourself Key, too, don't you?"

"Only because he does, because I've always known that that was the way it was pronounced."

"Well, that's why I do my way." Quy took a swig at his jug. "You still haven't got out of a child's habit of asking questions you know the answers to. Your father regards me as something of an embarrassment to him. I suppose I have been at times. It wouldn't be so bad for him if our name was Smith and Jones, there'd be nothing to connect us. But with an unusual name like ours, it's different. Especially as our paths have come close—not to mention crossing—several times since he started to make his own career."

"He says it's an old French name. He says that my great-great-great-grandfather fought in the American War of Independence with Lafayette."

"So he did, boy. Well, it was one more *great*, I think. And *with* implies a rather more exalted rank." He chuckled. "What—the Conte de Quy?" He pronounced it the French way himself now. "No, he was a private soldier, son of a peasant. He settled in the States when the war was over. His grandson, *my* grandfather, was of less heroic mould. He came to England to dodge the Civil War draft. Set up as a pastry cook in Liverpool and built up a prosperous business—which *my* father promptly drank into bankruptcy."

"That's not quite the same way I heard it from my father."

"*Ach*, what are we talking about the past for, anyway? Heredity's bunk. That's what Henry Ford said about history. It's nurture, not nature."

84

"But how about the families that several generations made names for themselves? Like—well, the Huxleys?"

The old man snorted. "That could prove nurture as easily as nature. Geniuses can have idiot children and idiots occasionally have geniuses. A man's what he *is*." He downed his beer. "You're on your own. So you get off home now and start studying. I'm going to stop and have another one."

The boy got up reluctantly.

"But—you will let me know as soon as the . . . you know . . . arrives."

"Course I will, son. Course I will."

Ten

The letter arrived two mornings later. He tore open the envelope and tried to read the letter, his fingers, to his acute annoyance, trembling so that the words jigged before his eyes.

"We . . . pleasure . . . awaiting . . . costing . . . however . . . completion . . . £225 . . ."

What was this? He sat down and anchored the letter to the bench with a tripod.

"We have pleasure in informing you that your order has been satisfactorily completed and that the specimen is awaiting collection at our main office. However, accurate costing (details of which will be rendered with the specimen) shows that the terminal cost figure of 10,000 £ was reached shortly before the specimen was completed.

"However, we proceeded to completion, and beg to inform you that a small sum of £225.8s is outstanding on

*the account and will be payable on collection, or against
pro forma invoice should you wish delivery.*
Assuring you of our best . . ."

"The *bastards*!" Quy swore. How much did he have
about the place? Which meant in the world. Forty, fifty
quid? And there was the printer to pay for the press invitations, not to mention transport and drinks. Journalists
were a thirsty lot, from what he knew of them. Of course,
he could always try—

But he had barely started to dig in his pocket for
coppers for the phone before he killed that line of thought.
Maggie had done enough. He wasn't going to go back to
her this time without the prize in his hands. He had even
decided, after soul-searching, not to invite her to the trial.
He couldn't bear that, if it should turn out a failure.

What was he thinking of? *Failure?* Letting a mere
two hundred quid deflect him now after all he had surmounted? He rummaged among his belongings and found
what he was looking for. He started to change, then remembered something. He looked in the mirror.

His hair looked like a patchwork rug of ginger and
white. He grimaced, threw on a jacket and went to the
Greek barber up the road. He came out with a crew cut
—the only way Nick was able to eradicate the second
color.

Back home he donned his best shirt and suit, then set
off down Caledonian Road. He knocked at a door halfway
down, made a request and waited patiently while Tiny
Bradford put a clean shirt on too. He felt better with that
six foot three of brawn—even if it was running to fat after
a five-year retirement from the wrestling ring—beside him.

They took the Tube to Piccadilly Circus, and walked
up Regent Street. The receptionist rang through and
showed them to a seat. A few minutes later the scholarly-
looking young man came out of a lift and across the
marble floor to greet them.

"Ah, Mr. Quy. Just come this way, will you?"

He looked a trifle surprised when Tiny got to his feet
too.

"One of my men," explained Quy. "One has to keep in with the union. I felt it advisable to come myself for this, but it does come under the heading of Deliveries and Collections."

Past a bronze door, the floor changed abruptly from marble to concrete. They went down a ramp that opened into neon-lit acres, with a loading bay beyond. They brought up at a counter. A snap of fingers and a brief word and a brown-coated attendant departed into recesses beyond. He emerged with a flat package and a sheaf of papers in a folder.

Quy took the package and tore at the tape at one end. He fumbled open the packing and drew out what was inside.

It was a dull blue in the harsh light of the neons. It looked like nothing more important than a scrap of board from a carton for washing powder or lump sugar. But the old man's hands began to tremble and he hurriedly stuffed it back in its wrapping. He handed it to Tiny.

"Now, what about this two hundred and . . . what was it?"

"And twenty five pounds, eight shillings to be precise."

"We must be precise." Quy took out a check book and a pen whose cheap alloy finish he hoped would glint sufficiently like gold. He wrote a check, tore it out and handed it over.

"Well, that's taken care of. Thank you for everything, Mr—what did you say your name was?"

"Gregory."

"Gregory. I will remember that in my future dealings with your company. You have given me good service." He took the folder and pumped the young man by the hand. "Come, Bradford." And he was halfway up the ramp when Gregory called out, "Just a minute."

Gregory came hurrying up. "You've filled this in wrongly."

"What's that?"

"You've filled in two *fifty* five."

"Have I? Oh, keep the change for yourself, Gregory."

"But—"

"You mean, the firm won't allow that?"

"I mean, the words say the right sum, the figure differs. It wouldn't be passed."

"Let me look at that. Why, so I did. A slip of the pen, old chap." He altered it and handed it back, but he was cursing to himself that the stratagem had failed. A wrongly written check would simply be returned to drawer for replacement. But a dishonored one—and there was no reason why it should be honored at a bank where he hadn't had an account for ten years—was a different kettle of fish. If he failed to replace a wrongly written one, that was only a matter for debtor's court—and he knew his way around *them*. But a dishonored check was a matter of . . . ugly word . . . *fraud*. He had never had that proved against him. And fraud was a prison offense.

They came out into the roar of Regent Street's traffic.

"Two hundred nicker for a bit of cardboard?" said Tiny in his deep slow voice. "That's a lot of money, Mr. Quy, ain't it?"

"West End prices, Tiny," Quy said blandly. But he brooded as they walked down Regent Street towards the station. He brightened. "Wait here," he said to Tiny.

He went into the post office and filled in a telegram form.

BIOTECHNICS, REGENT STREET. QUERY COST FIGURES. HAVE STOPPED CHECK IMMEDIATELY PENDING CONSULTATION MY ACCOUNTANTS BEFORE DEPARTURE AFTERNOON FLIGHT USA. WILL INSIST ON CONFERENCE IMMEDIATELY ON MY RETURN EARLY 1974.

Let them sort that one out! he said to himself as he handed the form in at the counter. Then he went out blithely into the Piccadilly Circus sunshine.

"Come, Tiny. We've done a good morning's work. I think we'll take a taxi home."

Eleven

The day dawned bright and blue. When he got back with the van he had hired, Alan was waiting on the doorstep, camera in hand.

"It's loaded," the boy said excitedly. "Only black-and-white film, though. I couldn't afford color."

"That's all right, son. Now, give me a hand getting this on the wagon, will you?" He went to one end of the contraption and groped under the tarpaulin for a hold on the angle iron. "Ready? *Heave.*"

Only one end lifted—Alan's.

"Come on, lad—it'll be easier as soon as we get it out in the alleyway. We can use rollers then. Ready again?"

But this time he straightened quickly with a yelp.

"Blast the damn thing! What price anti-gravity? *Norman!* Where are you?"

A ginger head poked out of the window above them.

"Coming right down, Mr. Quy."

Half an hour later, with the aid of planks borrowed from the builders' yard down the road; they had it on board and lashed fast.

"Right," said Quy. "We've got to hurry. We've got to be the other side of Epping by eleven o'clock. Can't keep the press waiting. You're the youngest and healthiest, Alan. You can sit in the back and watch the precious freight doesn't come adrift. You, Norman, ride up front with me."

They climbed in and set off.

By the time they had covered the mile to the Nags Head, Norman was sweating hard. It had taken them twenty minutes—a testimonial to the thickness of the traffic at that hour of the morning rather than to any sedateness of old Quy's driving. In between jams he reacted like a long pent-up spring, engaging gear ferociously and hurtling into the next snarl of traffic, arriving with a screeching of brakes.

At the Nags Head, the junction with the main trunk artery to the M1, he got into the wrong lane and got stuck across the traffic. The air rapidly became blue with diesel fumes and the imprecations of lorry drivers. One of the latter got down from his cab and stalked across to the van. When he saw Quy at the wheel, he gave a kind of frustrated sigh, heaved his great head disgustedly and guided the van free, with several inchings forward and jerky backings and bellows of "Full lock now," and "Left hand down now, Christ I said *left*!"

"Let me take over," Norman pleaded as they got under way again.

"*Take over!* Whatever for? I haven't driven a vehicle of this make before. I'm just getting the hang of it."

As he spoke, the van lurched out to avoid the back of a bus whose indicators were flashing and which pulled out just as the van drew alongside. Norman caught one look of the driver's startled face, and covered his own with his hands. There was a blare of horns. Then he was thrust back fiercely into his seat. When he opened his eyes the van was hurtling into comparatively open road.

"See!" said Quy triumphantly.

"Pull in," said Norman weakly. "I think I've got a call of nature to make."

"You should have gone before. Anyway, we'll be hitting open country soon."

"We'll be hitting *something*," Norman muttered. At the next holdup he switched the engine off and took out the key.

"Well, all right," said Quy crossly. "There's one just over the road there, next to the pub."

"That was only an excuse," Norman informed him. "This is an ultimatum. Either we change seats and you let

90

me drive the rest of the way or I get out and you can lug your own flying machine onto the launching pad. I've got too many adventures of Anthony Hard to write yet—and I never realized until this moment just how precious that could be to me."

"Are you sure you can drive properly?" Quy enquired.

"Give me that wheel," Norman snarled and shoved the other to one side. Quy submitted grumpily and contented himself with intermittent and largely irrelevant advice for the rest of the way.

They arrived at Wileys Green, an open space bordering Epping Forest, at ten twenty.

"Ah, there's the Blue Boar," said Quy. "Pull up there. That's the place I put on the press invitations." The van ground to a halt. "Funny, where are all the cars?"

Only one red sports car and an old gray van with a flat tire graced the forecourt. The Blue Boar had obviously seen better days.

"I know," said Quy, climbing out. "There's a big car park round the back. I remember the place well."

He came back almost immediately. "It's locked. So is the pub."

Norman looked at his wrist. "They won't be open till half past, I suppose. But it's a bit off the beaten track, isn't it? It's been B roads for the last twenty minutes."

"Nonsense. This is a famous pub. Or used to be. I think we must have turned off too early. I know the main coast road is only a mile away. That's why I chose the place. It's accessible, yet not too densely populated."

"You can say that again," said Norman, looking about him.

"Still, the invitation said eleven," said Quy cheerfully. "We can't expect the rush yet. The press are busy men. So it behooves us to be ready for them. Let's get the van over to the far side of the green and set the machine up. Then you can come back here, Norman, and greet the scribes. Here's a fiver, but watch how you go with it. Those lads can mop up scotch like sponges."

They lumbered across the green and got the machine

down. Norman left, while Alan checked his camera and Quy had a last-minute run with the generator and radio control. As he moved the controls of the transmitting box, the motor obediently speeded up, then slowed. He walked a hundred yards away and repeated the process. He could hear that it worked. He came back and brought the radio control to zero. The motor cut off immediately. All the same, he switched off manually on the machine before bolting in the precious blue strip.

"What's the time, boy?" he asked when the job was done.

"Ten to eleven," Alan told him.

"Fine. Now you stand guard while I go back to the pub. Whatever you do, don't touch it and don't let anyone come near it."

He set off back across the green. There was a blue Volkswagen in the forecourt. He went into the saloon bar to find Norman talking to a middle-aged character in a hairy jacket. The man had a spirit glass in his hand. He had a complexion that hinted that he had held many spirit glasses in his hand.

Quy's heart warmed immediately.

"Hah, press?" he exclaimed genially as he went up to them.

"Yep, I'm Arthur Fenton."

"Happy to meet you," said Quy. "If I hadn't dedicated myself to science, yours is the profession I would almost certainly have chosen. I'm Adolphe Quy, of course. My colleague—ah—" He suddenly realized, for all that they had lived in the same building for over a year, that he didn't know Norman's last name.

"Burroughs," Norman filled in quickly.

"No relation to the great Edgar Rice?" the reporter enquired, gazing into his empty glass.

"Not that I know of," said Norman.

"Great man," said the reporter nostalgically. "Cut my teeth on him. Barsoom and all that, eh? Galloping across the desert on a *thoth* under the orbs of Phobos and—what was the name of that other moon."

92

"Deimos," said Quy. And hurriedly, "Have another drink. What paper did you say you're from?"

"The Times."

"The Times?" Things were brightening. *They* reported things properly. The paper the Top People read. He could see it now—in a half-dozen of the top board rooms a hand would lift, turn over the pages, and stop. It would reach for the telephone. "Smithers, what's this I see about a revolutionary new kind of—"

Fenton interrupted his fantasy, killing it in mid-flight. "The *Mid-Essex Times*. Here's my card."

Quy took it and read it. "Arthur J. Fenton. *Mid-Essex Times and Epping Advertiser*. Correspondent for the London Press." But it didn't say which papers of the London press, and Quy didn't feel it was worth bothering to ask.

"The *Echo* forwarded me your invitation, seeing that it was in my territory."

Quy felt his elation ebb away, leaving desolate salt flats. Less than thirty miles from London, and one paper, at least, couldn't bother to send one of their own men. As for the rest—

The door opened and a young woman, in a dazzling black-and-white suit and a strictly urban blonde hairdo, came in.

"I'm looking for Mr. Adolphe Quy," she said in a Knightsbridge accent.

"That's me."

"Oh, good. I'm from the Globe."

The tides of hope came running in again. The Globe was a leading London evening paper.

"What'll you have, young lady?"

"I'll have an Orient Express, thank you."

"A what?" said mine host who was taking a puzzled, if gratified, interest in the unusual influx of visitors.

"That's a vodka, grenadine, and Campari."

"We don't have any grenadine. Or Campari."

"Just give me a straight vodka, then. A large one." She turned to Quy. "Now, Mr. Quy—that is how you pronounce your name, is it? Or French style—Key? Come and sit down over here and fill me in with some personal details."

Two vodkas later, Norman said, "It's eleven thirty, Mr. Quy."

"Time enough yet, Norman." The old man turned back to the blonde. "But, of course, my most notable—" He broke off. "What *is* it, Norman?"

Norman spoke hoarsely and urgently in his ear. "Our friend over there is beginning to get sloshed. He's on his fifth double whisky now. And there isn't a sign of anyone else."

"All right," Quy sighed. He was beginning to enjoy the company of the blonde. He turned back to her. "We have to get started on the demonstration now, my dear."

As they came out of the pub, Quy saw a large dark-green van pulling up on the other side of the green.

"Come on," he hollered and went trotting away over the grass.

"You see!" he said as he drew up, puffing but triumphant. "It's the B.B.C."

He spoke to the technicians.

"I think you'd better move the van away as far as you can. The demonstration won't be dangerous, but we'd better take proper precautions. Now, your cameraman had better take up position at the edge of the woods there. There's a bit of a bank. We can all get down behind it."

The blonde, Fenton and one of the BBC men looked the machine over.

"Briefly," Quy told them, "this is simply an ordinary generator. But it powers a strip of special anti-gravitic material in the base. If you'll just look under? I'm not at liberty yet to divulge either the composition of that strip nor what exactly happens when a current is passed through it. Suffice it to say that it works by screening off the power of gravity, with the result that this machine will rise from the ground. Just observe that there are no moving parts— apart, of course, from the generating unit. No airscrews, no jets, no rockets.

"Right, shall we take up positions?"

He switched on the manual switch on the sled and they trooped over to the edge of the woods.

"Right?" He nodded to the cameraman. "Get that zoom lens ready. Okay, Alan?" He moved the controls. The petrol engine started up, with a puff of blue smoke. "Now, there won't be a count down. I'll just say one, two, three, on. Ready?"

He prayed to a god too undefined for any church to have ever worshipped, and said, slowly and quaveringly, "One . . . two . . . three . . . *on*."

He activated the radio control. Fifty yards away a whine came from the generator and leveled out.

And nothing happened. The sled remained motionless on the grass, apart from a slight vibration from the generating unit. Or it might have been heat haze.

The seconds passed. Quy felt sick. "What's up, Prof?" called the cameraman.

"Wait," said Quy. "The field's got to build up." He didn't know how true that was, but if it was going to build up it should have done so by now, surely. "Just keep your camera on—"

Suddenly the machine lifted. It was two hundred feet up and traveling fast before he recovered enough to work the radio control. The thing suddenly went into an arc. *It must have turned over*, he thought desperately, *a lateral effect*. And then the machine was plummeting dangerously near to the TV van. He juggled with the controls and, with a scream of air, the thing came cartwheeling over their heads.

They all ducked, its inventor included, but he turned up power to the full as he did so. When he raised his head, the thing was streaking up into the sky, an eastward component in its trajectory. A glint in the sun, and then it was gone.

"There!" Quy shouted triumphantly. "It worked. You all saw it!"

Norman was white-faced; so was Alan, under his tan. Fenton was green. The cameraman's legs were trembling as he straightened. Only the girl seemed unshaken.

"Very impressive, Mr. Quy," she said. "I'll phone in a full report. I hope my paper will find room for it."

"Thank you, my dear young lady," said Quy gallantly. He turned to the cameraman. "Did you get it?"

"Dunno. Hope so. I did my best to keep my camera on it."

"How about you, Fenton?" asked Quy. "Where—?"

But Fenton was being sick in the undergrowth.

Twelve

Not possessing a television, he went down to the Swan which had one in the private bar. But the news came and went with no mention of the demonstration.

"It's early yet," said Norman, who had accompanied him to the pub. They bought a late extra *Globe* from a passing vendor. But he was shouting of a crisis in Pakistan and, though they scanned the paper through to the classified ads and out the other side, there was no mention in the *Globe* either. They waited till the nine o'clock bulletin.

"The crisis is easing in Pakistan," it started. It went on to the visit of the Turkish Prime Minister, the latest on the latest unsolved murder, a protest note handed to the American Moonbase commandant by the Russian Moonbase commandant, the Miss Universe eliminators, and it was getting down to the bottom-of-the-page stuff. Then, "That is the end of the general news. Here are the close of play scores in the county cricket matches. Lancashire—"

Quy turned to Norman and sighed. "Well, that's it. I've had a heavy day."

"Wait till tomorrow," Norman said quietly. "There's the *Echo,* and the *Globe* probably passed it on to their morning paper, the *Sun,* if it was too late for them to give it a proper write-up."

"Only three turned up," said Quy. "And I sent over fifty invitations. Who am I trying to kid?"

In the morning he was waiting on the local news agent's doorstep. He bought the *Echo* and the *Sun,* then—just in case—every other morning paper.

He found a paragraph at the bottom of page five of the *Echo.*

"Flying Machine Tested. Anton Quey, 71, demonstrated a new type of flying machine today at Wileys Green, Essex. It operates on an entirely new principle, claims the inventor. It is apparently some kind of hovercraft, without visible propellers or jets. The demonstration was only partially successful. After rising from the ground, the machine got out of control and was soon lost to sight. The craft was unpiloted and there were no casualties."

The old man felt suddenly sick of it all. Not a mention of anti-gravity. *Hover*craft! They hadn't even got his name right. Just as well, probably, if that was all the publicity he was going to get. There was always danger from a lurking creditor whenever he lifted his head above ground.

He scanned through the others. There wasn't a line. He would never know how loyally or not the blonde kid with the posh voice had implemented her promise to give it a full write-up. He fancied that she was a good kid under all that manner. She had probably rung in screeds to her desk. She was also probably a very junior reporter and it had gone straight into the wastepaper basket.

No hand would lift in any board room now, that was for sure. He sat in his shadowy room, wondering what the hell he could do next, when there came a sound of ringing, faint and faraway. It rang a few times before it penetrated his gloom. He leaped up and hobbled down to the callbox.

"Canal 5262," he said.

"Mr. Adolphe Quy?" It was a young woman's voice.

"Speaking."

"This is the B.B.C. We're ringing you because we

thought you might like to know that the news item which you so kindly acquainted us with is being televised in our Nineteen-Five program this evening."

"Nineteen five?" He was all adrift. What was she talking about the past for? His invention was of today—the future.

"That's the time it's on, Mr. Quy. Seven five P.M. It's our early evening topical interest program."

"Oh, I see. Thank you, miss. It was very kind of you to ring."

That evening he went down to the Swan in good time— alone. Norman had popped in to tell him, soon after the phone call, that he had just got a telegram from the editor of *Torso* to report immediately. It must have been an assignment, because he hadn't returned.

He had to switch the TV set from one of the other channels—to the anguished protests of an old hag who said she wanted to see her favorite serial and that was all she came in the pub on a Tuesday for. A senile skirmish in the sex war threatened until George, the landlord, intervened in Quy's favor. The old girl sniffed, drank up her Guiness and departed, leaving Quy the only occupant of the bar.

When the program started, Quy, with a disturbing sense of uncertainty, wondered whether he had got the B.B.C. woman's message right after all. The opening shot was straight out of nineteen hundred and five, a flickering sequence—obviously an ancient newsreel—of a birdman jumping to his death off a bridge.

The next shot was of a ridiculous flapping-wing machine of a similar vintage which went round in circles before collapsing.

"Man's dream of flight," said a smooth voice. "Those were just two examples of men's early attempts. The air-screw machine of the Wright Brothers was already a reality when those two shots were filmed, the main path to the skies already laid down.

"But there are always the pioneers, the restless ones, men who look ahead to new ways of conquering space."

There was another shot, of a primitive helicopter bucking up and down without clearing the ground, finally disintegrating under the fury of its own frustrated efforts; then one of a thing with fifty propellers along the top of it, which had about as much chance of flying as a sow in farrow.

"Some hopeless, some—" there was a still of an early rocket plane, hardly bigger than a child's firework—"that contain the seed of the future." Rapid shots of a jet plane and then the fulmination of a space rocket launching.

"Yesterday our cameras went down to Essex to film a demonstration by a veteran inventor." There was a shot of the Blue Boar, then one of the machine. Of himself, loping across the grass, and of the rest of them. Back to the machine and the reporters looking at it. "Is this the shape of things to come?"

The old man writhed. What were they trying to do? Didn't all early models of anything look ramshackle?

"Or—" There was a shot of himself with his hand on the radio control. Another shot . . . Christ! did I look as hopeless as that . . . *feel* as hopeless as I looked?

The camera just caught the machine, suddenly, blurred, at the top of its first flight upwards, then the landscape pitched crazily; the next shot was of the sled hurtling toward the camera. The landscape tilted again, there was a split-second shot of himself, a flash of Alan's face—good, the boy was holding *his* camera up—then the world tilted again, it was all sky, and that was that.

The shots were replaced by a studio shot of a face, the owner of the smooth voice, talking.

"Or just another hopeless dream? And now—the Pakistan crisis and its aftermath . . ."

Quy drained his glass and went back to his basement. That was it—no conclusive proof of anything. People had become too case-hardened by faked pictures of flying saucers and things like the "landing" on Mars a couple of years before which had turned out to be a publicity stunt for a film. People were too ready with other explanations. They'd prefer to believe in mass hypnosis rather than a real discovery. He had explained to them on the spot that the machine weighed several hundred pounds, that there had been nothing that could possibly have lifted it except some new motive power. But the world had got past being able to believe that a new discovery could be demonstrated in a field in Essex by a lone inventor. It was all launching pads nowadays and government publicity.

Alan turned up the next day with a projector and screen lashed to his bike.

"I got them processed as soon as I could, AQ. I got one better shot than they got on that TV program."

He set up the screen in AQ's room. Norman was back from his assignment—it had been to interview a Mexican python wrestler off the Queen Elizabeth at Southampton —and he came down to watch.

There *was* one better shot. The boy's quick reflexes had caught the machine going up. There had been a slight tremor and a jerk at the moment it took off. The film tracked it to its first peak. He had missed it there, though, having tracked on into empty sky. He had caught it up as it had hurtled over their heads—he *had* stuck to his guns —but the machine only showed up as a blur across one corner of the screen. It could have been a bird, anything.

The screen flickered and went white.

"Thanks, son," Quy said. "You did well." But he didn't look very happy.

"What's up, AQ?"

"It's not enough."

"But the TV program, the report in the Echo, *this*. I know they're not a lot, I know the paper and the TV program got the facts wrong or distorted them, but put together, they prove that *something* happened."

"They don't prove anything. And who's going to be bothered even starting to add up? As for the few people who saw it with their own eyes—I never bothered with Christianity because I thought that if all those people had seen what happened, there wouldn't have been just twelve apostles, but hundreds. I'm not so sure now. The human

100

eye has got marvelous powers of self-deception. No, it's not in the eye—the mind, or somewhere in between. People see what they want to see. And they refuse to see what they don't want to. The ostrich bloody complex."

"I'll put an article together," said Norman quickly, "and try and get my editor interested. It's not their normal cup of—"

"Thanks, Norman," Quy said wearily. "But do you really think an article in that kind of magazine would be any help?"

"It was just a thought."

"No—I've got to start all over again. My God!—old women die and leave a fortune to a dog's home. They raise fifty thousand quid, easy as kiss your backside, to put up a monument to some crooked politician. And here—I've got this . . . and what use is it to me or anybody?

"Ach, what's the use of talking? Leave me alone. Go back to your typewriter, Norman, and do some real work. Let somebody be producing something that somebody wants." He wheeled on Alan. "And you get back to your books, d'you hear me? There're enough failures in the Quy family."

He slumped down and bowed his head in his hands.

Norman looked across at Alan with a pained, helplessly sympathetic look on his face, then softly opened the door and was gone.

Alan stood there, looking down at his grandfather.

"I—"

The old man looked up.

"What, haven't you gone yet?" His voice was suddenly vehement. "Bugger off!"

The boy flinched as if he had been slapped across the face. And his face was suddenly as red. He turned abruptly and stumbled out of the door.

Quy did not stir for some moments, then a look of sudden grief seized his face. He propped himself to his feet and saw, as he moved to the door, that the boy had left his movie equipment behind.

101

He went out into the yard, but the bike was gone. And the alley was empty in the August glare. He rushed out into the street, but there was no sign of the boy. He shrugged. He would be back.

He stopped by the callbox, hesitated, then went in and dialed a number.

No ringing tone came immediately, then there was a click, a brief ring and a voice said, "Park Mansions."

That was odd. It was entered as a direct line in the directory. But he jabbed button A.

"Lady Wentworth, please."

"I'm sorry, her ladyship is away. This is the porter. All calls have been switched to the switchboard. Can I help you?"

"How long will she be away?"

"I'm not sure, sir. Her ladyship is away on a cruise."

"But you must know when she'll be back. I—"

"I'm sorry, sir, that's all the information I can give." And the line went dead.

He cursed. But he came out of the callbox feeling almost relieved. But where else was he to try now? He couldn't go back to Biotechnics. They had probably put his file in the hands of their legal department by now. And he had exhausted every other company that could conceivably do the job.

But it was more than a strip of the material he needed now. There was no point in rigging up another demonstration in the middle of nowhere. He had to harness it properly. He had proved the Quy Effect—at least to himself. His lips freaked in a bitter smile at the name. *The Quy Effect!*

But a strip *could* be enough. It had been arrogance on his part, he recognized now. Or fear that the credit for the one great discovery of his life would be filched from him. But to hell with that! The discovery was the important thing, not the bloody glory. And he could protect himself, all right. He should have done it this last time, taken the strip to one of the big firms and let them test it

102

under their own selected conditions. They'd have to believe it then.

But now he needed another strip . . . another ten thousand pounds.

For a moment he had a wild idea of haring over eastern England, seeing if he could find out if something had dropped out of the skies. Perhaps, right at this moment, a scrap of something that looked like blue cardboard was lying in somebody's backyard.

He dismissed the idea with the contempt it deserved.

But somewhere there must be somebody. *America.* They were more go-ahead there, more ready to look at new ideas, more money to spend on crazy-looking projects without having to worry whether more than one in a hundred turned up. Ten thousand quid—how much was that in dollars? Anyway, it would be peanuts to them.

But he had about ten pounds left in the world. That wouldn't see him very far across the Atlantic. *Fly Now, Pay Later?* You had to have credit standing for that.

And his own was at an all-time low.

Thirteen

He spent the next couple of days brooding impotently, feeling that life had shriveled to a heavy acid lump in his guts, wandering, rubbing shoulders in cheap cafes, on park benches, with the other failures of the great city.

He came back home the second evening, lingering by the canal. He looked down into the oily black waters that the rays of the sloping sun seemed to shun.

Down there under the waters must be the detritus of many hopes. Rusted iron that had once been shining machines, losing race tickets, programs of theatres that had long since closed their doors, old boots, contraceptives, a lonely body or two that nobody had ever bothered to look for.

All buried now under the easeful anonymous slime.

He shivered and turned away. When he got back to his basement he found somebody waiting for him in the yard. It was Preston Quy.

"Hello, son," the old man said dully. "Why didn't you go in? The door's open."

"I did. I soon came out again. Where's Alan?"

Quy noticed now that his son's face was grim.

"Alan? I haven't seen him for a couple of days. Why?"

"He's missing from home."

"I see. But that's rather a drastic phrase, isn't it? He's just gone off somewhere for a few days. You know what kids are."

"I know perfectly well what kids are. Better than you possibly could. I also know my own son. He often goes away on the spur of the moment in the holidays or at weekends. But he always leaves a note or telephones. Two evenings ago, he came in, didn't say good evening to his mother or me. When Doris called him for his supper he was just gone. So was his bicycle. I know he came to see you that day. He had a film. That's his projector inside, isn't it?"

Quy nodded. "Oh, he's probably still brooding on his exam results, that's all."

"I don't think so. He seems to have recovered from his disappointment. I'd made arrangements for extra tutoring for him."

"Well, that then. You're worrying over nothing. He goes back to school soon, doesn't he? He's just making the most of his last days of freedom."

Preston snorted angrily. "It's more than that. What have you been saying to the boy? I know he's been seeing a lot of you lately."

"He told you that?"

"I can tell. I can always tell. I know you've got some

104

scheme or other on foot. I know he went with you on that so-called demonstration. I saw that piece about it on television."

"Did you now?"

"Doris says he was all excited when he went out that day. He told her he was going to pick up the film. Now just what happened in a few hours to make him change so abruptly? Is he doing something for you?"

"No. Not that I know of. I didn't ask him. No, there couldn't be anything."

"You don't sound very sure."

"We-ell, he knew I needed money."

"That's nothing new."

"Perhaps. But I don't think Alan, with all the will in the world, could have imagined that he'd be able to raise ten thousand pounds."

"Ten thousand?" Preston Quy lifted his eyes to heaven. Then he shook his head disgustedly. "What an influence on a boy his age! Wild schemes, haring after crazy dreams. What have you been feeding him?"

"Nothing. Nothing bad, if that's what you mean. Now son, I've been tramping miles and my feet are aching. I'm going in to sit down. If you want to come in you're welcome, but I'm not going to stand out here in the yard arguing with you."

He turned and shuffled into the dim interior. Preston hesitated, then hoisted his shoulders and followed.

"Right, then," he said, picking the least dilapidated chair. All the same, it creaked under his weight. "What happened that day?"

"What's this—the third degree? He came here with the film he took of my demonstration. He showed it. Then . . . well, all right, I suppose I was a bit short with him. He left pretty abruptly. But he knows me—if anyone does. He knew I was fed up."

"How short? Come on—let's have it."

"I told him to go back to his books."

"I bet I know the way you told him to do that!"

"All right, Press, have it your own way. But I've never

105

tried to deflect him from his studies. What do you think —I want to set him some kind of shining example? I know myself a bit better than that. I may talk a few ideas with him. Some of my ways of looking at things—ones perhaps you don't agree with—might have rubbed off on him a bit. But nothing bad for him. A kid's got to equate the world about him. He shouldn't take it all out of books and teachers' mouths."

"There—I knew it!"

Quy cursed himself for saying the wrong thing. He always seemed to, speaking to his son. It was like a demon in him. He added quickly:

"But I've always told him that he's got to learn what's in the books first. I haven't tried to undermine his teachers' authority—or yours." He suddenly remembered. "But some weeks ago, just after he knew he'd failed his exams, he told me that you had your mind set on him joining you at the Ministry. He didn't like the idea of working on weapons."

"I don't care where he works. He can make his own mind up. I just want him to do something worthwhile, not go around the way he has been these past few weeks."

"I told him to join you, if that's what you wanted. I wouldn't want to wish my kind of life on anyone, least of all a kid."

"You can say that again," said Preston, looking about him at the dingy, chaotic room. "My God, what have I done to deserve this? I've always tried to make things right for my family, for Alan, for you even. If I was going to have a problem father why couldn't I have had just a simple alcoholic, like other people, or a helpless dependent? Not somebody you couldn't help even if you tried?"

"All right, son, don't carry on. You won't do yourself any good. Alan will be all right. He's a sensible kid. He knows what's in his power and what isn't." He sniffed. "Which is more than I ever did, I suppose. No, he's just gone off somewhere to work out his future course. As for me, I'm sorry."

Preston stared at him suspiciously. "That's the first

106

time I ever remember you using those particular words."

"Yes, I'm sorry I haven't been a better father to you, instead of somebody you're ashamed of." He waved a skinny hand. "No, you needn't deny it. You've had enough grounds. I'm a failure. No, not even that. If I'd been a failure I might have recognized the fact earlier, got reconciled to it the way millions of other people have to. But I couldn't even manage that properly. I'm a half-failure—a strange twilight beast—somebody always doomed to be on the edge of success and never get there. I—"

"*Please,* father. Don't speak like that. There aren't that many true successes in the world. But, look, if you've given up all your big hopes at last . . . say I make you an allowance? Not a lot, I can't afford that. But I've just had a few hundreds salary increase. Enough to see that you live better than this. You've worked hard enough at your ideas, whatever I may have thought about them. You've earned some kind of a pension. But on condition that you don't tinker about any more, don't go around talking people into parting with their money. I *want* to help you. I—"

"Then help me in this. Look, Press, I've made the big strike at last. A man doesn't know what shape his life is taking, what it's all in aid of. But I do now. I've discovered the biggest thing since—since God knows when. Since atomic energy, anyway."

Preston shifted uncomfortably in his chair. "Here we go again! You mean, that thing I saw on television?"

"Yes—that thing you saw on television. That was the first flight, however primitive, of an anti-gravity craft."

"Oh, not—"

"You say *Cavorite* this time and I'll—"

"All right, but anti-gravity in that sense is still an impossibility."

"All right, in that sense it is. But in any other sense? It breaks Newton's Third Law of Motion? Got any other objections?"

"That's enough, isn't it?"

"That doesn't start to be enough. Just because every

107

human method of propulsion has been by reaction against something else, is that any proof why it has to be a universal law? There's no inherent reason why the power of a self-contained unit can't be transferred directly into movement of that unit—if only we know the trick. Mankind's got to find that trick or stay marooned on his own little planet for the rest of his existence."

"We're already on the Moon. Soon they'll get to Mars. We're not exactly—"

"What, on those bloody deathtraps they use now? All right, but how far? And at what cost?"

"You didn't talk like that in the thirties. I may have been only a kid, but I remember the way you used to carry on about rockets and the conquest of space."

"I gave them up, didn't I?"

"You thumping old—" Preston broke off, and sighed. "Look, dad, are you trying to kid yourself now? You know you gave them up because the Germans were obviously way ahead."

"Nonsense. I realized even then that they weren't the answer. Rockets have got about as much future as the dirigible airship had. A certain beauty, a kind of glamour, but too damn dangerous and cumbersome and expensive. Riding space in a pint-sized canister on top of a thousand tons of high explosive—that's not the way. We've got all the energy we want, if we can only use it. We shouldn't have to rely, in this day and age, on crude chemical reaction. Subject a man to ruinous accelerations because we have to carry a giant-size gas tank a minimum distance. What we need is more like a nuclear-powered submarine. Point its nose in the air and *float* up."

"Simple as that? They're working on atomic rockets. Ion drives, laser adaptations."

"*Pah!* That still involves chucking stuff out the back. Reaction mass. So you've still got to get rid of that mass as soon as possible. You're still going to have your acceleration stresses, which is going to limit the kind of people you can send up, the *number* of people."

"They're working on that, too. They've got—" He

stopped abruptly. "That's top security. It's not my department, anyway. But I can tell you they've got teams working on all these problems."

"Anti-grav?"

"Any kind of propulsion that'll get them into space easier and better."

"All right then, Press. It may not be your department, but you're a pretty important man. I've got to the stage where I'm beating my head against a wall. I can't afford to wait any longer. You put up my discovery to 'em. You—"

Preston looked pained. "I only chat with a few people in the space program. We meet at parties. Sometimes we exchange information in committee. But—"

Quy was suddenly angry. "You mean you won't? All right, I tried to make peace between us. I thought that this way I could redeem myself. I'd even forego the credit. How much farther could I go than that? Put it forward as your own idea." He laughed shortly. "Of course, they'd never believe that! So perhaps you've got reason."

Preston skirted the sarcasm. "Put it forward yourself. On your own. You don't need my sponsorship."

"Hah, I can just see that! *Passed to you for your attention.* *What's this? Anti-gravity? Put it in the special file; you know, the one for crackpot ideas.*" Finishing up as just another folder gathering dust somewhere in the vaults of Whitehall. No, thank you very much."

He got to his feet.

"I'm sorry if I embarrassed you, Press. I'll find somebody somewhere. There must be a firm somewhere in these benighted islands that—"

He broke off. "*Firm?* What am I talking about?"

Preston looked nervously at his father, then recognised an expression that had been familiar to him, on and off, since childhood. One that meant that there was no point in discussing anything any further. He got up too.

"I'll be off, then. Don't forget what I said about—"

"All right, son, all right," said his father.

But he wasn't listening.

Fourteen

After some initial research he wrote three letters. Within a few days he received three form letters beginning "Dear Sir, We thank you . . ." going on, "We regret . . ." and finishing, "However we will keep your application on our register, and should . . ."

He sat down and wrote two more, exhausting his short list.

The next day there was a knock at his door. He opened it to find a big man in a blue raincoat standing on the doorstep.

"Mr. Quy?"

Quy's eyes flickered over the visitor.

"Who?"

The man consulted a notebook.

"Adolphe Quy."

"Never heard of him."

"Who are you then?"

"What's it to do with you?"

The big man grunted heavily. "All right, what are you doing here if you're not the occupant?"

"I've been sent by the landlord to clean this place up after the last tenant."

"Was his name Quy?"

"How the hell do I know?"

"What's the landlord's name and address?"

Quy improvised quickly.

"Canal Estates, fifteen—" he broke into a short fit of coughing—"fifteen Finsbury Pavement." That was near enough for the other to follow it up now and not make it any more awkward for him at the moment—and far enough to afford himself time to take evasive action. "Now, if you'll let me get on with my work."

The big man wrote in his notebook, gave Quy a last suspicious look and departed. Quy went back into his basement, then after a few minutes came out, a moth-eaten carpet bag in his hand. He proceeded to lock the door with a large old-fashioned key, then went upstairs to Norman.

"I've got to leave rather hurriedly," he explained. "I just had a visitor who's a bailiff if I ever saw one. I managed to duck this time, but he'll be back. Not that I've got anything worth seizing, but I know what the follow-up will be. Will you alert the postman, make sure you get any letters addressed to me?"

"Certainly, Mr. Quy. That'll be all right. But I'm sorry to hear the news. Where shall I forward the letters to."

"I'm not sure yet. I'll let you know."

He caught the train for Brighton. The place he was looking for was a bus-ride out of town. He got there to find a haughty female who told him that applications had to go before a committee, that she could tell him now that there wasn't a vacancy at the moment, but that they would keep his application on file.

He thanked her with more civility than he felt and rode back to the town.

It was the end of the season, but the town was full of day trippers. Why didn't he drop everything right here? There must be plenty of odd jobs going. Washing up in restaurants. Caretaking. He could walk along the sea-front on his days off, in white shoes, chat to the old dears. Perhaps find some widow with a nest egg. *Come to Seaview. Mr. & Mrs. Adolphe Quy, Proprietors. Personal Attention.* Kippers for tea and bingo every Wednesday and Friday.

He shook his head and took a bus to the station. There he made enquiries and caught a train to a little town he had never heard of, called Uckfield. From there he took a bus to Tunbridge Wells. The sun had been set for a long

111

time, before, three bus changes later, his limbs cramped, he arrived at Midbury.

He came out into medieval streets. His few fellow-passengers—it had been the last bus—had evaporated, leaving the place deserted under the light of a swollen harvest moon. His footsteps rang on the cobbles as he set off in search of a bed.

He soon gave up. The town had put up its shutters for the night. He settled for a bus shelter. The nights were getting cold now, but he was tired out and he soon fell asleep.

He awoke at dawn, had a wash, shave and brush up at a public lavatory, left his bag at the bus station and set off for his goal.

He passed the soaring cathedral on the way, and black-and-white Tudor houses, but the University was all bright brickwork and modern statuary. He found his way to the bursar's office.

The woman behind the desk here was a carbon copy, tweeds and all, of the one at Sussex University at Brighton.

"Mr. Osborne? We received your application yesterday. You couldn't have got our letter already?"

"Letter? Ah no, I happened to be in the neighborhood, so I thought I would look you up."

She reached into a drawer and brought up some papers.

"Well, we do happen to have a vacancy for a technician, grade two, in our Biological Laboratory. But—" she looked at him quizzically—"aren't you rather—er—" She met his fierce gaze and looked down at the papers. "You say you're fifty-seven?"

"That's right."

"You realize, of course, that there could be no question of superannuation."

"I'm not worried about that," Quy told her cheerfully. "I'm well provided for. I haven't worked for several years, as you see from my references." The "references" and the identity were ones he had used when he had infiltrated Preston's department. "But with the current shortage of

112

skilled workers I thought I should put the national need before my own motives."

"Well, since you're here, we can soon find out whether you'll be any use to us." She pressed a buzzer, and shortly afterward one of the uniformed figures Quy had seen at the gate entered the room.

"Oh, Rogers, this is Mr. Osborne. Take him across to Mr. Herd in the Biological Department." She scribbled on a card. "And give him this."

"Thank you, madame," Quy murmured. He followed Rogers across a flagged quadrangle, past something that looked vaguely like a chapel—it had a concrete spire standing next to it, anyway—and into a large building. They finished up in a small office. A thin-nosed man in a white coat looked up and read the card that the porter handed him.

"Mm-mm. Thank you, Dave." He looked at Quy dubiously. "Let's see if you know your way around." He led Quy into a vast, gleaming laboratory. "What's that?"

"An autoclave," Quy answered without hesitation.

"This?"

"An electron microscope."

"And this?"

It was like a large safe set into one wall. There was an observation window in it, beneath which were set a pair of what looked like openwork metal gauntlets. Through the porthole he could see a pair of metal arms.

"A radioactive chamber. This is a biological laboratory, so it's probably used mainly for radioactive isotopes."

Herd's thin face cracked into a frosty smile. "Good. I think you'll do. Can you report for duty tomorrow?"

He hadn't done such a humble job in a laboratory for years. Clad in a brown coat, he autoclaved specimens, renewed the contents of bottles and racks, made up solutions, cleaned test tubes—and even swabbed floors.

And was happy.

He soon became an accepted part of the surroundings. The young men and women, mainly, seemed to like him.

113

He was probably a change, at that, he reflected, from some ham-fisted kid. He found comfortable lodgings in the town. He even began to put on weight.

The only slight snags were technical ones—like the whereabouts of his national insurance cards and tax papers. He hadn't been very careful about those in his right name; he had none at all in the name of Osborne. He told the office they were on the way, and after two repetitions of the query they left him alone, deducting the cost of a stamp every week and putting him on temporary tax coding. Which meant a shrunken pay packet, but that was the last thing he was worrying about. If anything, it lent substance to his claim that he had private means. He got enough to get by on . . . and he was laying his plans, finding requisition forms, external order forms, practicing signatures.

He let Norman know his new address—and his new name. But it was not until October that a letter came for him bearing a N.1. postmark. He smiled in distant gratitude for the fact that Norman had re-enclosed the letter and had even covered the name and address on the original envelope inside with a thick white label.

The letter was from Alan, the envelope postmarked Scotland.

S/C 12467
Craigmyle Depot
West Lothian
Scotland
5th October 1973

Dear AQ,

Sorry to be such a long time letting you know my whereabouts. But I couldn't let anybody know until I was sure that I was here to stay. I had to forge dad's consent to get in here.

Quy smiled ruefully. That made two of them.

114

I had a long long think about things. It wasn't dad's work: I just realized that I wasn't cut out for a desk job—or a bench job, come to that.

Dad was hopping mad when I let him know. He threatened to have me out. Which he could have done easily enough in the circumstances. But he came up here and we talked it over. He must have seen how happy I was, because he gave way in the end.

Happy! I must be crazy. They get you up at O-six thirty hours and the day starts with a brisk half-hour's P.E. Then it's lessons, more P.E., lessons—then a spot of P.E. for a change. Next week we start un-armed combat. Don't ask me what that's got to do with it.

Hope you're finding a way to perfect the Quy Effect.

Your loving (a word X-ed out, but it looked like grand-) sidekick, Alan

P.S. S/C stands for Space Cadet, of course.

"I'm finding a way, son," Quy murmured. He started to write a reply, but couldn't find ways of explaining what he was doing, why he was here under a false name, with-out complicating things or worrying the boy. He had chosen his path. Funny, but he *had* got into uniform after all—and he felt a nostalgia for his own long-distant youth and the way one's views changed so rapidly then. But if that was what the boy wanted, he could do without distractions from *him* for a while.

He went on laying his plans, getting books and papers out of the University library, wangling requisitions. By the end of the winter term his plans were complete. He took the final steps carefully, telling Herd that since he had no relatives or friends to go to for Christmas he would come in and get everything in order for the new term. Word must have got around, because two of the students invited him to their respective families for the holiday. He politely declined, but his heart was warmed.

A few of the postgraduate workers stayed behind to

115

finish up experiments, then they too were gone, and the whole big shining building was his.

Now he marshaled everything to its place—near the cat-cracking furnace. The books, the electron microscope, the tanks, the materials. That took him two days—for he had to keep to normal hours for fear of arousing suspicion with the skeleton staff of porters and maintenance men.

And then he was ready. This was only going back to Square One, preparing another batch of the superconductor. But with that in his possession there was hope. He began to assemble the long and complicated molecule, using techniques that he had picked up when he was with Hypertronics and in three months study here. He was in a new universe—his own private universe . . .

He was brought back to reality by the sound of footsteps outside. He straightened hurriedly, switched off the furnace and the electron microscope. He was making his way to the sink, rolling up the sleeves of his brown coat when the doors were flung open. In the doorway stood Rogers, Herd, and Miss Cairns, the woman from the bursar's office.

"What's going on here?" Herd demanded.

"How do you mean? I was just checking equipment."

"I don't think so," said Herd grimly, taking in the unusual disposition of the apparatus. "I've been doing some checking myself these past twenty-four hours. One of the men in another department thought he recognized you from somewhere. I discovered the books you were getting from the library."

He strode to the bench and turned over the pile of books there. "Odd reading for a mere technician, aren't they? Then there were certain appropriation forms I couldn't account for. All right, what's the game, Quy?"

The old man's air of injured innocence evaporated.

"Very well, you've caught me in the act. And you know my real name. I was just doing some private research. It won't have cost the University much."

Herd was going round the laboratory.

"Is that right, Mr. Herd?" Miss Cairns asked.

"It seems so. I think we got here in time. The appropriations only amount to a hundred pounds or two at the most, and they're things that will probably come in useful some time. He hasn't damaged any of the apparatus. He's no fool with that, but it beats me how he ever thought he could get away with it."

"He might have if it hadn't been for your quick action."

"Thank you, Miss Cairns."

"All in all, as long as we've discovered it in time, I think we can consider the matter closed. Perhaps we can lock the place up now and get some peace. Mr.—whatever your name is—kindly regard your employment by this University as closed forthwith."

There was nothing else for it. Quy took one last regretful look about him, then he took off his brown coat and was shepherded out of the building and toward the gate by Rogers.

As he passed the concrete chapel he heard the sound of voices raised in song. It must be local school kids rehearsing, by the sound of them. It was only when he was being escorted out through the gates that the words impinged, and his lips freaked in a smile as bitter as they.

"In the bleak mid-winter . . ."

Fifteen

He came out of Charing Cross station. It was the day before Christmas Eve, and the streets were full of shoppers. He started to elbow his way to a phone box, then changed his mind and hailed a taxi. At the seventh attempt he got one.

"Three two five Clargies Street," he told the driver.

117

Maggie herself opened the door to him.

"Surprise!" He tried to smile. "What's this, staff shortage?"

"Sophia's gone home to Italy for Christmas. Come in, you look frozen stiff."

She took his overcoat, looking sadly on him, and led the way into a fireless drawing room. "Sit down. I was just leaving. The Hon. Mrs. Keld-Horsham has invited me to Christmas on her Hampshire estate. The spirit of the festive season, and all that." She prattled on, somewhat nervously, as she went around plugging in electric fires. "But I think that before it's over she's going to ask me if there's a place on the board of Wentworth's for her husband. I'm afraid she's going to be disappointed."

She brought over two glasses of scotch. She handed one to him.

"Happy Chr—" she began, and stopped at the look on his face. "Ah well, the old year will be over in a few days' time, so say we drink to the new one right now."

Quy nodded dumbly, raised his glass and gulped at the whisky.

"It's all right," said Maggie. "I can guess why you've come. So I'd better say here and now that it's impossible, Ado. I just haven't got the money." Her laugh wavered briefly between apology and bitterness. "I know that sounds like the rich person's traditional excuse. But it's true. I haven't got all that much money of my own. It's all tied in with the company, in trusts and that kind of thing. If I died tomorrow, the accountants would wrestle with figures for six months and finally arrive at a statement that would show that I was a millionairess. But, living, I have to go over my checks every quarter with them, and if I—"

"It's all right, Maggie. You don't have to justify yourself with me. You've been more than good. I did come here looking for more money. I'm past pride now. God knows I never had very much when I needed money for anything. But I had to try."

118

She looked at him for a long moment. Her next words were at an odd tangent. "How's your wife, Ado?"

He looked at her in puzzlement, indignation almost, as if fancying that in some obscure way she was trying to confuse him.

"She's dead," he muttered. "Didn't I tell you? She died over ten years ago."

"No, you didn't tell me. You also didn't tell me, fifteen years ago, that you had one, but—"

"To hell with you, woman!" he said savagely. "What are you trying to do?"

"Just making sure, Ado. I can't let you have any more money." She hesitated. "But I'll marry you. And I'm not losing *my* pride now. Just taking you up on an old offer that you weren't in a position to implement then."

"Go on, reproach me! As if I haven't enough—" He stopped short. "You'd do that? After all I—?"

"On conditions."

"Conditions? What, that I dress respectably and—"

"Nonsense. You know how to dress yourself. You've got all the social airs and graces tucked up that sleeve of yours, when you want to use them. Though heaven knows when and where you picked them up." Her face softened. "No, Ado, provided you just stop burning yourself up. Enjoy your last few years in peace. You could—"

"You mean—drop all my work?"

She nodded.

He laughed bitterly.

"My son offered me the same thing. Stop everything that means anything to you and I'll give you a weekly allowance."

"But it's only for your own sake, dear. God knows how a conniving old rogue like you can inspire such affection, but—"

She got to her feet and paced the room, her arms folded, one hand plucking at the sleeve of her expensive suit. She wheeled on him.

"*Pride!* You may show it in a peculiar way, but you've got more pride than any man I ever knew! Arrogance is probably a better word. I'm not doing you any favors, and you wouldn't be doing me any. For your own good I wouldn't give you another penny for your so-called research. Face it, Ado, you're past it."

He got to his feet now, trembling.

"Past it! Michelangelo was designing buildings when he was over eighty. Verdi wrote Falstaff when he was seventy-nine. Goethe——"

"*Verdi? Goethe?* When were you ever that interested in music or literature? What have you been doing, reading texts of consolation for old age? All right, we all read what we need, I suppose. But they were already famous, they'd already laid the foundation. At your age it's too late. I don't want to be cruel, you poor dear old bastard, but *face* it. Take what you can get when it's offered. God knows I haven't got anything better to do."

"Thank you."

"I meant that literally." Her voice was very quiet. "I can't think of anything I'd rather do."

He drained his glass. "Thanks, Maggie. But I can't accept it. Don't think I don't appreciate it. But I've got to go on."

He went back to his basement. He had sent his rent to Norman to pay for him, so he had legal rights to somewhere to lay his head—if the bailiffs hadn't taken up occupation since he had last heard from Norman. But he hoped they had cooled off by now. And he had a few pounds in his pocket.

It was dark when he entered the passageway. He went up to see Norman first.

"Hello, Mr. Quy. Come in quick. Here, have a drop of the hard stuff. Got it in for Christmas."

"Not just now, thanks, Norman. I haven't worked up the mood for festivities. But why all the 'Come in quick'?"

"You tell me. You've had several visitors this past day or two."

"Bailiffs? Police?"

"I don't think so. Though I can't have had your experience. No, there were a couple of foreign-looking characters. They've been sniffing around more than once. Then this afternoon there was a man I think I've seen here before. Civil Service looking type. Bowler hat and dark overcoat and all."

Quy felt relieved. "Sounds like Preston. That's my son."

"Thought I detected a resemblance."

"Could you? Wonder what he could want."

"No idea. I kept clear. He had another man with him, an older man."

"Perhaps it's somebody from one of the Ministries. I offered my discovery to my son, you know. He turned it down then. Perhaps he's changed his mind."

"I thought you hated government departments, the way I've heard you talk."

"I do, Norman, I do." He sighed. "But I've come to the end of the road. I don't care as long as my discovery gets used. Ah well, I'd better go along and get the place aired."

"Sure you won't have that drink?"

"I don't think so, thanks, Norman. But I'll have a drop of milk, if you've got it to spare. Think I'll brew up some tea."

He went downstairs, clutching a half-filled bottle of milk in one hand and his carpet bag in the other. He fumbled in the bag for his key and let himself in.

The basement smelled cold and dank. He shivered. He had never noticed it before. He switched on the light. They hadn't cut that off, anyway. He plugged in a fire, then lit the Bunsen. He swilled out his water can, filled it up and put it on the tripod. He was just hunting in the cupboard for tea when there was a knock at the door. He shuffled over and opened it.

His son stood in the doorway, more silhouetted against the darkness than illumined from within.

"May I come in?"

Quy held the door open wider for him. Only then did he notice the other man with him, who followed Preston in. This must be the older man Norman had mentioned.

"This is Dr. Stapledon," Preston said.

121

"Oh, yes. From the Ministry?"

Preston and the other man exchanged glances.

"No, not exactly. Sit down, father, we want to have a talk with you."

"Well, all right. I was just going to brew up, but it can wait." He turned the Bunsen down. "Yes, what is it? If it's about my invention, I've decided that you can have it. We'll discuss—"

"It's not your invention we came to discuss," Preston said, his voice oddly flat. "It's *you*. I got wind of your dealings with Biotechnics. That's a euphemism. I had a private detective call on me. You may be used to that kind of thing happening to you, but I'm not. I came to a decision. That decision was reinforced early this morning when I had a phone call from Midbury University. About a certain J. K. Osborne whom one of their staff had thought they recognized as Mr. Quy."

"I'd change your name to Smith, then, if I were you," Quy told him.

"It's a bit late in the day for that. Or for you. No more false names or false identities. I tried to help you one way. Now it'll have to be another. Not the way I would have preferred, but there's no other alternative. You've forced it on me. Believe me, I'm only doing it for your own good."

"*My own good!* You're the second person today who's told me that. What did I do to get surrounded by a lot of do-gooders? I don't want anybody worrying about 'my own good.' Not only don't want—I'm not going to let anybody. I may be down, but by God, I'm a free agent still. There's nothing you can do about it, so—"

"You're wrong, I'm afraid. There is. Dr. Stapledon here—"

"*Doctor . . .*"

Quy wheeled on the other man, the significance of the title impinging. He had assumed that, being with Preston, he was a doctor of science. But now—

"I have given Dr. Stapledon full details on your past

conduct. He thinks they form sufficient grounds. And your behavior now—"

"*Certified?*" the old man screamed. "You can't get away with it, you—"

"That's not a word we like to use," Stapledon said hurriedly. "You'd make it easier for everybody, yourself included, if you agreed to become a voluntary patient."

"*Patient?* What for? What am I supposed to be suffering from?"

"Do you want me to answer?"

"I wouldn't bloody well ask you if I didn't."

"Very well. From what your son has told me, I should say schizophrenia, paranoia, mental incapacity. I quite appreciate that these may only be symptoms of undue stress, but they seem to be a recurring pattern. At the very least, it seems essential that you be removed from a disturbing environment and—"

"Disturbing environment? Is that what you call it? Liberty's a very disturbing environment, isn't it? If you think I'd sign any of your forms and become a voluntary anything you're the one who's out of his mind."

"Well, the alternative is what you call certifying, but which we call committal. I have full powers to—" He jumped to his feet. "Now, now, Mr. Quy. Violence will only prejudice your case."

He was between Quy and the door. He backed away as Quy came at him, brandishing a wrench snatched up from the worktable, but still barring his way to the door. The wrench swung, catching the doctor a grazing blow on the cheek. He yelped. Quy raised the arm holding the wrench again and shoved with the other.

"Stop him!" Preston shouted.

Quy flung the door open and stumbled out into the yard, hollering like mad. Out in the alley, he made for the main road beyond. Footsteps came thudding after him. He turned wildly and flung the spanner. There was a tinkling crash of glass. Then everything was confused. Somebody grabbed him from behind. A dark shape loomed

123

up in front of him. There was a grunt and the grabbing arms fell away.

Other hands tooks him—round the shoulder.

"Mr. Quy? Quick, with us."

He didn't question; the world was going crazy around him. He let himself be led along—almost carried—a short way. A car door closed behind him. An engine started up. Lights flashed past the window.

Slowly he got his breath back.

"Who are you?"

"Your friends—I hope. You are Mr. Adolphe Quy?"

"Yes."

"Good. It would have been unfortunate if we had made a mistake. We want you to come and work for us."

Quy was conscious now of the slight accent. "Us? Who's *us*? What are you—foreign agents or something?"

The shadowy figure by his side laughed softly.

"That phrase has a wide meaning. A commercial attaché is a foreign agent, isn't he? In a way, Mr. Quy, I suppose you could call us foreign agents. But not in the manner of your James Bond."

"You seem to be well on the road—body-snatching in dark alleys."

"We knew you were in all kinds of trouble, Mr. Quy. We were ready to help in less melodramatic ways. Pay your bills, etcetera. We've been digging into your background. We know who your visitors were. We had to move quickly." The man's face was briefly, garishly illuminated in the neon light of an advertising display. The glimpse gave Quy no clue to the nationality of his companion. "But you're not being kidnapped. We can easily drop you back home, if you say the word. Though we hope you won't. And I don't think you will. That was a very distressing conversation we overheard."

"You mean, you had the place—?"

"Of course," said the other, almost apologetically.

"What government are you working for?"

"We're not working for any government—directly."

"Silly question, I suppose. All right—what country are you from? It's not *them*, is it?"

The smile was evident in the man's voice. "No, it's not *them*."

"Then who?"

The man told him.

"We think you may have the answer to something we've been looking for. In our space program."

"I didn't know your country had one."

"Not many people do. Ordinary people, that is. We're on record. We've managed a few rockets, a couple of satellites. We decided several years ago that in orthodox techniques, rocketry, we couldn't begin to match the big powers, so—"

"Match?" Quy was beginning to get things into some kind of perspective.

"Our researches are peaceful, if that's what you mean, Mr. Quy."

"That's what *they* say. What *we* say. What they all say."

"Do you want to go back?"

"No, keep driving—for the time being, anyway. Whereever you're driving to."

"Oh, to nowhere in particular. Not until you agree to our proposition, that is. But if you want straight answers to straight questions, that's not so easy in this world. But I'll ask you a question. Has the possession by the major powers of moonbases upset the balance of power? Has it made nuclear war any more likely?"

Quy thought of Alan. He must have asked himself the same question before he had decided to join the Space Service.

"No, I don't think so. I never did think that control of space would give any advantage in that direction. If any side could *get* control. It's a big place. Anyway, they'd reached the ultimate in destructive power right here on Earth without having any missile-launching platforms on the Moon or anywhere else in space."

"Very well. Then we come to the central question—do you think that your discovery, if perfected, could upset the . . . ah, apple cart?" The word was haloed by a foreigner's pride in using the idiom.

"There again, I don't know. But how did you find out about me? What makes you think I've discovered *anything*? Anything practicable, that is. Nobody else seems to believe me."

"Nor do we—necessarily. But we're ready to try to. We can't go in for expensive programs, so we've looked elsewhere for our answers. Our people have felt that somewhere there might be a simpler—a less cumbersome—solution to the problem of space. We've had a world-wide intelligence service checking on any kind of lead. On our budget that's a whole lot cheaper than the cost of just one rocket.

"The lead to you came from a short cutting in one of your newspapers. We checked back and found that there had been something about it on television. That was all there was—and all we needed. And here we are.

"And here you are. We haven't got all the time in the world. Although you are far more precious to us than to the other people seeking possession of you—and our reasons more worthy?—they will soon be taking steps to track you down. We want you to fly to our country and work with our people. Now—yes or no?"

"But I don't have my passport on me. It's back at my place. It's out-of-date, anyway."

The figure by his side chuckled.

"Don't worry your head about such small details, Mr. Quy. That's all been taken care of."

Sixteen

University of Tel-Aviv
Israel
2nd December 1974

Dear Alan,

How's this for a turnup for the book? I'm sitting on a balcony, overlooking the purple-blue Mediterranean, dictating this letter to a very pretty Girl Friday called Rebekkah. I'm beginning to appreciate the benefits of a team. Rebekkah is smiling.

Excuse me for not writing earlier. Things got pretty desperate, one way and another, back in England. I don't know whether you heard anything from your father. But the least said about that the better. Except the next time you see him or write to him, tell him that I recognize that he was trying to do what he thought was right. Don't worry about what that means, just pass on the message. Don't tell him where I am, just that I'm well and happy and not to worry about me any more.

I haven't written sooner because I wanted to get everything straightened out—and to let you get things straightened out. I got your letter telling me that you had joined the Space Service. I hope you are finding that it's your right path. I'm sure it is.

Well, I never thought in my life that I'd ever get any closer to Israel than the Whitechapel Road on a Sunday morning. Least of all be working here and enjoying it. My work is state-supported. They've got their own bureaucracy out here. But it's a different kind of bureaucracy. You're never remote from the man who makes the decisions.

Ther are committees, but small ones and informal. And I guess that I'm kind of an honored person around these parts. A patriarch yet! They respect old age here. You don't have to holler your head off to get attention.

I failed to produce any more of the molecule back in England. Though I nearly succeeded with a last surreptitious attempt. I produced it here—or my team did, with me breathing down their necks—three weeks after we got the equipment together. And while the lads were testing it I was tinkering about modifying it.

This is the place for experimenting. Old men and new ideas—they've got plenty of time for both. They've still got a working model here of an organic engine they developed years ago. It was never a commercial proposition, but it's a handy thing to keep in the locker against the time that the oil gushers in the states next door cease to gush. It's basically a synthetic muscle, fed by alternately contracting and relaxant chemicals, to drive a piston. People who can dream up things like that don't think there's anything strange in using an organic molecule to achieve the Quy Effect.

This project is not directly under any government office—except the Treasury. But you'll appreciate that there's a certain amount of security around it. And there are signs that it's thickening up. And even I can appreciate the wisdom of that. But it lacks the flesh-creeping elements of the big bloody nations and blocs. This project is for pride, not power. Still, I can't talk too much about it.

I can tell you, though, that we're licking the problem of controlling the Quy Effect. Oh yes, the name you gave it is the one used here—if nowhere else yet. No signs of Ivan or Wang-Fu over the horizon yet. But at least there's proof here of precedence. So your old grand-dad has a good chance of making the history books yet. Not that I care a damn about that—but it's a nice thought to have at the back of your mind. I'm too busy working on the Effect to worry about anything else. It's getting to the engineering stage now—and I don't mean angle iron and army surplus.

Just taking a day off to write a few letters, then it's down to the beach with Rebekkah.

I'd better put 'Read and Destroy' on this. But, before you obey the second injunction, just let me say again that I hope you're following your heart's desire and—though I've never been a religious man, here in a country which is a place of pilgrimage for several . . . even the Muslims, did you know that?—I feel I can say, God bless you, son, and keep you.

> Your grandfather,
> Adolphe Quy.

> S/C 12467
> Craigmyle Depot
> West Lothian
> Scotland
> 8th December 1974

Dear AQ,

Delighted to hear the news. All R & D, let me assure you. I can't say a lot about my work either, though I'm still at ground-level yet—in more ways than one. But I'm happy here and passed my first year exams with what I think, with all due lack of modesty, I can call flying colors. If I tell you that they flunked out over half the lads, you'll understand my feeling a bit cocky about it. And more than a bit sad at losing some good buddies.

Soon I shall be moved on. Don't know where yet—and if I did I couldn't tell! But I'll let you know as much as I can when I can.

> All best,
> Your loving grandson,
> Alan.

P.S. I told dad your message—on the phone. He said sorry too for what he did. Don't know what that means. Poor old dad! But he's much more philosophical about things these days.

> University of Tel-Aviv
> Israel
> 8th September 1975

Dear Alan,

Move heaven and earth to get here next month, 15th latest. Tell your C.O. or commandant or space patrol leader or whatever, any story you like. I'm about to give birth—but you'd better not tell him that! I've informed El-Al, the Israeli airlines. So wherever you are you can pick up a ticket from their nearest office. But make it, whatever you do. You'll have a story for your buddies.

AQ

University of Tel-Aviv
Israel
8th September 1975

Dear Maggie,

Hear an old man's prayer and fly to Tel-Aviv just as soon as you can—by 15th October latest. I don't want money this time. Only your presence, and I want that more than anything else in the world. I can't say any more now. But remember I said once that I wouldn't come to you without the prize in my hands. I broke that promise twice, but this time I'm making good on it. I'd come running with it, only this prize is a bit too big to carry. So Mahomet will have to come to the mountain. *Please*. And please let me know that you've received this letter. It's very important to me, believe me.

Yours ever,
Ado.

OCTOBER 8 75 9.00 M.T.

WENTWORTH ENGINEERING WESTERN AVENUE PERIVALE MIDDLESEX ENGLAND. VITAL I CONTACT LADY WENTWORTH IMMEDIATELY. PLEASE INFORM. RETURN PAID. QUY. TEL-AVIV ISRAEL.

OCTOBER 9 75 6.30

CABLEGRAM M.V. AUGUSTA COMSATT AREA 1. I WROTE YOU LETTER WITH MOST URGENT REQUEST YOU ARRIVE HERE FIFTEENTH LATEST. PLEASE COME. TURN SHIP AROUND IF NECESSARY. ADOLPHE QUY.

OCTOBER 9 75 7.00
COMMANDANT SPACE SERVICE ONTARIO CANADA. PLEASE
RELEASE SC 12467 GRANDFATHER ADOLPHE QUY CRITI-
CALLY ILL HERE AND ASKING FOR HIS ONLY GRANDSON.
TICKET CREDIT MADE AND AVAILABLE ANY OFFICE
EL-AL. KINDLY FORWARD THIS MESSAGE URGENT. FOR-
WARD RETURN PAID. TEL-AVIV GENERAL HOSPITAL IS-
RAEL.

Seventeen

It was all over now.

Now it was the turn of the mechanics, the mathemati-
cians, the doctors and all the other specialists whose
interests came to a focus a hundred miles away in the desert, thirty hours to zero.

The rest of the research team were out there. Quy sat
on his Tel-Aviv balcony looking over the sea, feeling alone
in the universe.

The telephone rang. He grabbed it.

"Rebekkah, Mr. Quy. I'm all ready to leave. The car
will be here in fifteen minutes."

"Catch it then, honey. Don't wait for me."

"But, Mr. Quy. Aren't you coming?"

"Not yet. They can get along without me."

"But—"

"Don't bother me." He slammed the receiver down.

Shortly after, there came a knock on the door and
Rebekkah came in, looking distressed.

"What's wrong, Mr. Quy? I can't leave you sitting here
like this. It's the big day tomorrow. You've got quite a few
formalities to get through."

131

"———the formalities."

"Mr. Quy! I don't know what that word means, but I'm sure it's nasty."

"Sorry, dear. Just reverting to type. I'll be there for the important bit. I'm in no state to go through any formalities. I'm likely to forget my manners with the President himself, the mood I'm in."

"Your friends mean so much to you? The Lady and your grandson? Very well, I will wait for them with you."

"They won't be coming. I would have heard by now. Anyway, the morning plane came in half an hour ago."

"Customs. Entry control, Mr. Quy. They're bound to be more thorough with something like this on. Shall I ring the airport? They can—"

The telephone rang. Rebekkah had a start of several yards and fifty years to it.

"Mr. Quy's apartment. Yes. Thank you. Yes, up here, please."

She turned to Quy, smiling happily.

"Well, is it?" he asked impatiently.

She nodded.

"Which one? For heaven's sake—"

Rebekkah went to the door and leaned her back against it.

"Blasted women!"

Then there was a knock on the door and Rebekkah moved aside to open it.

Quy was on his feet.

"*Maggie!* I thought you'd never make it." He took her in his arms.

"Nor did I," Maggie said breathlessly, disengaging herself to straighten her hat. "I was halfway to Bermuda. I was on a round-the-world cruise. Your letter wasn't forwarded. I practically monopolized the ship's radio for three hours, while the office back home got a messenger to my flat. They read the letter over to me. The captain was very understanding, but he couldn't turn the ship back. But he sent off radio messages like mad and we hove to— or is it heaved to?—in the middle of the Atlantic while I got rowed across by lifeboat to an oil tanker. They dropped me off at Gibraltar. I flew on to Athens, and—well, I'm here. But don't ask me to go through *that* again."

"You look as if you've just stepped out of Vogue, for all that," Quy said admiringly. She was dressed in a pale blue linen dress and a wide straw hat.

"And you look as if you've stepped out of—I don't know what—Playboy, I should think. *Tchk tchk.* Flowered shirts at your—"

She broke off, glancing at Rebekkah. Then she looked back at Quy.

"Oh, I'm sorry," Quy said quickly. "This is my secretary, Rebekkah. Rebekkah, this is Lady Wentworth."

The two women shook hands, rather warily.

"Now, Ado," Maggie said. "What is all this about?"

"It's a long story, Maggie. But I'd rather show you than tell you, now that you're here. Becky, is there still time to catch that car?"

Rebekkah looked at her watch. "Yes, just time."

"Right. Come on, both of you."

It was waiting in the driveway—a black Cadillac. Maggie raised her eyes appraisingly at it and at the uniformed chauffeur who opened the door to them.

"I noticed it when my taxi pulled in," she said to Quy. "I had no idea it was yours."

Quy chuckled. "It's only at my service temporarily."

They swept out of the city, past gleaming white and glass towers and date palms, out into desert country. They passed a camel train before they had gone very far.

"It's a land of contrasts," Maggie said. "Cadillacs, skyscrapers, and camels. And you, Ado. Two years ago you were on the floor. And now *this*. You look years younger." Her eyes twinkled. "For all the lack of hair dye."

"I felt years older than I've ever felt," Quy said softly. "This morning, before you turned up, Maggie."

She pressed his arm, then turned away to look at the miles of desert rolling by.

Soon they came to low hills. Rebekkah reached in her briefcase and brought out identification tags, with photographs, handed one to Quy and pinned one on her own blouse.

"You've got your passport on you?" Quy asked Maggie.

"It's here in my handbag."

"Good. You'll probably have to show it. We're getting near the security perimeter now."

They came through a gap in the hills, to a view of more desert beyond.

On the horizon was something that looked like a large encampment. But even from this distance it was obvious that this was no nomad camp, but a nexus of modern technology. Vehicles were moving between buildings and erections of girder and lattice on the perimeter, and a central cluster. Just what that central cluster consisted of was hard to make out, for the throng of vehicles about it and the mounting heat haze in the air.

They passed one armed guardpoint. The car stopped, but the guards waved them on immediately, without even querying Maggie's presence. Obviously, the fact that she was with Quy was enough. But at the next, and last one, her passport was scrutinized closely, and a few words were exchanged between the guards and Quy before they were allowed through.

And it was only beyond the second guardpoint that Maggie could get any clear view of the central object. She was none the wiser for it.

"What *is* it?" she whispered to Quy.

"*Sh-h,*" he said.

The car pulled up and they got out. Quy took Maggie's arm and led her towards it, passing under the shadows of what were obviously radar installations.

They came to within thirty yards of it. Maggie stared for a full minute, her eyes ranging over the strange shape. It was partly under covers.

"Well?" she said at last. "That's the craziest looking hunk of machinery I've seen for a long time."

It was about a hundred feet long, ovoid—and faceted. It gleamed silvery in the warm autumn sunlight, but certain of the facets were a dull blue. There was a port at one end of it, through which was visible a maze of machinery and dials and men working.

"Is this the same idea you were working on?"

He nodded.

"You don't tell me *that's* expected to *fly*?"

"I'm not sure that's the right word, but—broadly—yes. Why, what have I missed out? Rockets? Nose cones? Are they what you're looking for?"

"No, I'm just thinking it's pointing the wrong way—if something that shape can be said to be pointing anywhere."

"Ah—the persistence of an image! We've been brainwashed so long, haven't we? The long slim shape pointed upwards, the gantries. That's the flapping-wing equivalent of the jet plane. And dead as a dodo after tomorrow."

"The dodo didn't have any wings." She waved a hand. "Don't mind me. I don't know where I am at the moment. That five thousand-mile dash has just caught up with me, I think."

"Do you want to sit down, dear?" asked Quy, suddenly solicitous. "I'm sorry, I should have thought. The heat and everything."

"I don't faint that easily." She smiled. "Not even at this. It's just all so unbelievable, that's all. But there seem to be a few hundred people around here who do believe it." She wheeled on him. "Adolphe Quy, if this is your last and greatest confidence trick, I'll—"

Quy was roaring his head off. "That's another persistent image. No, this is it, the prize. At least, by tomorrow we'll—"

But she was already moving towards the ship.

"Hey, watch out for yourself!" Quy shouted, seeing a drab-clad guard reaching for his pistol. He moved quickly. "It's all right, officer. The lady's with me."

Maggie looked under the drapes, then came back, looking sad.

"The *Chaim Weizmann*."

"I know, Maggie. I'm sorry. It's not the *Maggie Wentworth*. I wanted that. But this is a small proud country.

135

They made this all possible. I couldn't say no. Even though, if it hadn't been for you, I—"

He broke off, looking miserable. Then a smile broke over his face. "But there's something I *can* name after you. Come on."

"But where are we going?"

"Back to town and quickly."

Eighteen

The Cadillac pulled up at a large white building in the center of Tel-Aviv.

"What's this place?" Maggie asked.

"The Municipal Center. Come on, I'm going to take you up on an offer."

"You mean . . . Ado, is this the old heart breaker? Where's the romance?"

"That can come after, love."

"No, it can't. I don't care however big the event may be tomorrow, you're not rushing me into marriage like this in a strange country. I'm not having my head shaved for you or anyone else."

"Come off it, Maggie, you know enough Jewish people to know that's not true. Only one very tiny orthodox sect does that."

"Well, whatever they do."

"It'll be a civil ceremony. Just a straightforward—"

Maggie had found the door catch. She was out of the car before he could stop her.

He stopped only to tell the driver to wait, then went after her.

"What is it, Maggie?" He was breathless. "Slow *down*. Now, what's it all about? This isn't like you at all."

"Let's go for a little walk, Ado, and talk it over."

Quy shrugged.

"All right, Maggie. Me arm, ma'am." They set off along the pavement. "Now, what's wrong?"

"Nothing's wrong, Ado. It's just so, so—"

He smiled tenderly. "Not—*sudden*? Not for us after all this time?"

"No, you old—" She sighed. "No. I'm the one to feel old now. When I said I'd marry you, it was—well, I was offering you peace, security. I—"

"That's all it was? Pity?"

"Of course not. All right, perhaps it was mostly pity, for myself as well. But things are different now."

"How?"

They were passing a café, with tables outside and striped umbrellas. She tugged at his arm. "Let's stop here. It'll be easier over a drink."

"All right." They sat down at a table. "What'll you have?"

"What are you having?"

"My usual out here. Vermouth and tonic."

She looked surprised, but said, "All right, I'll have the same."

They did not speak until the drinks came. Then they looked at each other over the rims of their glasses. He took a sip and then said quietly, "Now then, Maggie, come clean."

She seemed to have recovered something like her usual poise.

"Well . . . one. If it was pity on my part, isn't it now only gratitude on yours? No, don't say anything yet. Two, if this project succeeds, will you be satisfied, or will you still want to go on?"

He waited. Then his expression changed from patient expectancy to something more quizzical.

"Well, what else? One doesn't normally start numbering off for only a couple of objections."

"Not objections, Ado—questions."

"Questions, objections, whatever you want to call them. For the first, if you could offer out of pity I can offer out of gratitude. For the second, what's wrong with my not being satisfied with this, for wanting to go on? But are you sure you know *your* motives. Are you sure it's not been power over me you've wanted?"

"*Ado!*"

"I'm not being hostile. But are you sure you didn't help me in the hope—well, that this time he'd make such a mess of things that he'd finally see the light and come running back?"

"If that's what you think—"

She started to gather up her handbag. He placed a thin, but surprisingly strong, hand over hers.

"Come on," he said. "You're covering up for some other reason. Don't tell me—" he looked at her from under lowered eyebrows—"that you've got married again?" He roared suddenly. "I didn't interrupt you on your honeymoon?"

"Of all the arrogance! To think that—" But she could not hold back a chuckle.

It soon died. "But—oh, this is difficult to explain, Ado. I've been widowed getting on for twenty years now. You get used to a man—your relations with him. I don't mean Relations with a capital R—hark at me getting all coy!—but all the other little intimacies of a man and woman together. It's easy enough making the offer—"

"I asked you first."

"When you weren't free to carry it through. But let's not talk about that. Perhaps I was confident that I could marry again, if the man was—"

"A *failure*?"

"I wasn't going to say any such thing. No, somebody who possibly needed my help more than I needed his."

"That's pride, Maggie. I do need you. But I won't say that I'll ever settle down. You wouldn't want me to—if you want me at all. But I don't mind confessing that I've

138

got used to a more purposive existence. More comfortable. Free of worries. There's a middle way."

"It's done you good, too, Ado." She hesitated. "That's the real point. I wasn't being complimentary this morning at your apartment when I said you were looking so much younger. And that only made me feel older. Especially standing next to that secretary of yours."

"Rebekkah? Don't say you think—"

"I could see the look in her eyes. Another woman always can, you know."

"Nonsense." But his old eyes sparkled and his chest seemed to expand under the flowered shirt. "I never thought of that. We've had some good times on the beach together, but—"

"You see, that's what I'm frightened of."

He began to laugh. Then, seeing the look persisting in her eyes, he stopped abruptly.

"There was nothing like *that*. I admit she looks handsome in a bikini, and it's all very nice and flattering—but she doesn't look half as handsome as you do right now. Now, come on, I'm a man of influence in these parts, but offices don't stay open all day, even for me. What do you say?"

She didn't answer for a moment.

"You'll be losing a title, of course—or will you?"

"If you think that would worry me—"

"On the other hand, you'd be gaining a share in a name in the history of science."

"That too."

"Last chance," he said, but humbly, gently.

And she was nodding, smiling through tears.

Nineteen

The Cadillac came for them very early the next morning. The sun was red and low on the horizon as they traveled towards it over the desert. In his happiness, Quy hadn't thought about one particular thing. Now he remembered and he felt a dull ache inside him. Alan hadn't turned up. Now he would only hear about it, like everybody else in the world except the few hundred people associated with the project—from the papers and television of whatever part of the world he happened to be in.

If he heard at all. The Israeli government was unlikely to release news of the attempt if it was anything less than a success.

They arrived at the grounds. He showed the new Mrs. Quy round the ship and introduced her to the crew of four who were making the trip. One of them, to Maggie's surprise—another part of the familiar space image gone—was obviously in his fifties.

"It's because there's no need for vicious acceleration," Quy told her as they moved on. "He's the best man for the job. I tried to wangle a place myself." He smiled. "But I didn't have the right qualifications."

"Since when did a little point like that stop you?"

He smiled. "No, there *is* an age limit, even on this."

There was a noon luncheon, at which Maggie was introduced to the President of the Republic and various other dignitaries. A toast was drunk to the venture. The President performed a simple ceremony. The covers were removed from the machine. The crew entered, and the heavy port closed behind them.

Klaxons sounded round the area. Technicians at radar and TV screens answered final checks.

A guard came running up to Quy and whispered urgently. The old man gave a start, then nodded. A jeep set off across the desert. It was returning when the klaxons went again.

The jeep wheeled to a standstill, and a tall figure in mid-blue uniform stepped out of it and came across the baked sand towards them.

Quy had to turn away and make out he was intent on the centerpiece. It was such a far cry from the last time he had seen the lad. As this was from a village green in Essex and a handful of indifferent reporters.

"You're a fine one," said a voice in his ear. "I arrived on the morning jet and went dashing to the hospital. I had all kinds of horrible visions of what I would find."

"The hospital! But I left a message there for you."

"That didn't stop me worrying all the way from Woomera."

"So, that's where you were. My cable followed you half round the world. Sorry if I upset you. But I had to do something pretty drastic. I wouldn't have wanted you to miss this." He looked at the boy appraisingly. He had filled out a lot since he had last seen him. He had grown up. He nudged him in the ribs. "Have they got anything like this at Woomera?"

The boy looked at the strange craft in its cradle.

"No."

"Not yet, you mean," his grandfather said.

A low whirring started somewhere in the bowels of the *Chaim Weizmann.*

"That's the atomic generators starting up," Quy said. The ground trembled slightly, and so did the hand on his arm.

"Oh sorry, Maggie. This is Alan, my grandson. Alan, meet your new grand—Heavens! That sounds all wrong." He grinned. "This is MQ."

The boy blinked.

"We got married yesterday. We—"

141

A final klaxon went. A hush settled on the assembly. Through the observation port the men could be seen moving controls. Then a face looked out; a hand gave the thumbs-up.

Its movement was not unlike that of a rocket as it rose slowly. But there was no roar of detonations, no flaring of vapor from the sides, no cushion of flame. Just an eerie silence, accentuated, if anything, by the quiet hum of generators. Nothing in the history of mankind had ever stayed in the air like this before. Unmoving now, no part of it moving.

A bird hovering. A sail-plane. But even these drifted on a current of air. Nijinsky, they said, had managed to stay like this at the peak of his leap, some aching artistry of muscle and fiber nullifying gravity. But only for a split second. Then the fall.

But this held. And none of the watchers, the hardest-headed guard to the most intent radar operator, but felt the stir in him of age-old race dreams. And race aspiring. *This* was the enemy—and it was being vanquished. Not the symbol of brute conquest—as Freud had said, a sexual symbol . . . though the onlookers felt the ache of it in their loins like sex . . . but more than that, much more than that—the libido, the urge of man to throw off the mud of one planet. The dream in the seed that had driven men to martyrdom from cliff tops. Set man-made angels—pitiful mechanical simulacra—to fly in Santa Sophia in Byzantium. The craft began to lift.

As smoothly as a limousine it gathered speed.

Alan was gaping upwards. When he lowered his eyes for a moment from the light of the sun, he noticed his grandfather's fingers crossed behind his back, so hard that the knuckles were white against the tan.

He lifted his eyes again to see the ship gleam once before it disappeared from visibility. Only then did the cheering break out, then that too stopped as people crowded round the TV screens.

"When will it go into orbit?" Alan asked in a strained voice.

"Oh, in about thirty hours from now."

"*Thirty hours?* I remember you telling me that it didn't need sharp acceleration, but this is ridiculous."

"Round the moon, I mean," his grandfather said, beaming.

"*Wha-at?*"

"Well, you didn't think we'd be satisfied with a mere Earth orbit, did you? Rockets can do that. Personally, I thought it was too modest a target. I wanted Mars. But I'll be satisfied. They can go to Mars next time. And don't be so disparaging about acceleration. This thing can accelerate a damn sight quicker than your thunder-gutted ships. We don't *have* to, that's all. Of course, when it comes to interstellar flight—"

Alan was shaking his head dazedly, watching the pictures on the screen. "Everything's fine," a voice was saying. The face showed none of the strain of rocket pilots. "Handling perfectly. All systems go." The familiar words sounded strange in the different circumstances.

Adolphe Quy was standing there, one arm around Maggie's waist, still looking up into the sky.

But his thoughts were not on the ship. That was on its way. He was free of it now. The team could carry on. But the possibilities of that molecule weren't exhausted yet—not by a long shot.

Superconductivity meant that an impulse could be stored indefinitely, unwasting . . . a memory bank. It wasn't a coincidence that it was akin to the fundamental life molecule, DNA. Somewhere there was a clue here to what gave life its meaning. Its intelligence. In each cell. Like the way they had found that primitive creatures, nematodes, fed on their fellows, which had been taught to follow certain primitive directives, themselves following those directives. He had read it somewhere. He must check it.

And the fact that the body renewed itself so that in a few years the body, cell for cell, had been replaced, yet the intelligence—the identity—remained. *Whatever Miss*

T. eats turns into Miss T. It was hazy yet. But it would fall into place. Time enough—till tomorrow anyway.

He chuckled. *"Whatever Miss T. eats—"*

"What did you say?" Maggie asked.

"Eh? Oh, nothing." Then he felt a twinge of guilt in his new role of husband—until he realized that his fingers were still tightly crossed.

He uncrossed them. "Just thinking," he said.